1000 Home Based Business Ideas

Innovative Small Business Ideas For The Home Based Entrepreneur

ISBN 10: 1-4515-5436-2
ISBN-13 978-1-4515-5436-6

1000 Home Based Business Ideas

Innovative Small Business Ideas For The Home Based Entrepreneur

John Hanwall

"An amazing thing, the human brain. Capable of understanding incredibly complex and intricate concepts. Yet at times unable to recognize the obvious and simple."

Jay Abraham (America's number one marketing wizard)

Home Based Business ideas

If you're stuck for ideas on how to get some extra money in then you're sure to find something here. True entrepreneurs have the ability to take an idea and get numerous other ideas from it. If you can't find a nugget amongst the goldmine in front of you then forget about working for yourself – you'd be better off getting another job instead.

So, if you're ready, lets go . . .

1.   Begin a confidential newsletter about how to get the best things from life. The best things in this case include: money, expensive property, respect an quality cars. Your newsletter should suggest some of the legal short cuts which can be taken.

2.   Produce personalized reward charts for young children. You need to design a colorful template with a popular character or animal and include the child's name. For each order, have it printed on card or thick paper and laminate it. You could throw in a free felt pen or stickers.

3.   Start a service which writes persuasive monologues for individuals. For example, a C.V. designer helps a person get an interview, your service provides monologues for people to use at interviews. Or help people to get a date or to propose marriage.

4.   If you live in a busy road and you are at home all day, place a good looking sign outside you house stating that you do car washing and polishing. Also advertise that you give a personal service and that car owners can call at your house any time.

5.   Bring out a DVD which consists of a long recording of a moth or butterfly. By playing the video a cat owner cane keep their pet occupied for hours on a rainy day.

6.   Set up an agency which specializes in providing attractive men and women for sales and reception work at business promotions, conferences and exhibitions.

7.   Become a pets portrait photographer. You have to prove to potential customers that your portraits are far superior to any amateur photographs. This can be done by displaying your work on a stall in a public place and selling your service to people who take an interest in your work.

8.   Hire out: Window boxes, bottle gardens, exotic plants, tubs of plants and hanging baskets. Your clients will include: offices, banks, pubs, hair salons, restaurants, exhibitions, etc. Also provide your clients with a maintenance service.

9.   Make a wide range of electrical extension leads. Make extra long leads for people with large gardens, for business make industrial extension leads which are up to 1000 feet in length. Get shops and trade suppliers to accept orders for you.

10.   Begin a computing lesson of the month club. Each month send a home computing enthusiast a CD which gives instructions about how to use a popular application or how to improve their programming skills. Advertise in home computing magazines.

11.   Take top quality photographs of historic and well-known buildings in your town or region. Select the best photographs and have these printed on writing paper and envelopes. The idea is

that tourists will use this stationery to write home. Also do the same for other towns or regions.

12.   Start a craft business which makes a selection of cactus products. These products, such as paperweights, book ends, desk sets, etc. have live cacti growing out of them.

13.   Arrange for ink drawings to be made of historical characters from all parts of the nation. There might be hundreds of drawings. Have these printed and framed and sell by mail order. The idea is that wherever a person is, they can buy a framed drawing of someone famous from their own area.

14.   Produce an encyclopedia of self-improvement on audio CDs. This should cover all subjects related to self-improvement and might be 20-50 CDs in length. Sell in monthly installments or as a complete course.

15.   Design a log book for the house. This is to record every physical change to a house so a householder can: Analyze costs, plan future changes and have the feeling of being well organized Arrange for the log book to be printed and sell by direct mail to householders.

16.   Buy a candyfloss making machine. Sell your candyfloss from a site where there is a continuous flow of people who are enjoying their leisure.

17.   Put together a correspondence course about how to become a professional investment adviser. Sell through ads in the financial press.

18.   Publish a newsletter for those who want to make money from manufacturing kits. Kit manufacturing provides a spectrum of opportunities. Deal with all aspects of starting a profitable kit making business.

19.   Produce a series of audio CDs which contain quotes from the bible. The quotes on each CD might be selected according to a theme. For example: How to meet bereavement and sorrow, how to meet the challenges of everyday life, and how to live in harmony with others.

20.   Set up a mail order company which sells local history books. Put together a selection of local history books for most cities and towns in the country. Produce a catalog and sell through media advertising.

21.   Use sea-shells to make a range of jewelery, including sea-shell brooches, bracelets, earrings and necklaces. Place these on racks and have them stocked at suitable shops.

22.   Put together a hamper of Christmas decorations. In each hamper include all the decorations needed to completely decorate a room of average size. The packaging might include a picture of a room which shows where each of the decorations might go.

23.   Bring out a series of plans for woodworkers, soft toy makers, leather workers and other craft-workers Either sell printed copies of these plans at wholesale prices or sell the reproduction rights. Then any craft-worker or hobbyist can start a mail order business selling the plans.

24.   Design and make a selection of patchwork hats, caps, jackets, dresses, etc. Find retailers who will stock your products.

Or design and produce kits so that anyone can make their own patchwork products. Place classified ads in needlework magazines and sell by mail.

25.   Invest in a course of singing lessons. If others find your voice pleasing to listen to earn money from singing at pubs and clubs.

26.   Supply a fortune teller or numerologist for parties and weddings. A visiting fortune teller makes a party or wedding reception more entertaining for guests.

27.   Organize board game playing holidays and weekend breaks. Guests might play: the latest fashionable board games, etc.

28.   Make candid videos of weddings. Candid videos provide a fascinating, more accurate record of a wedding. Copies can be duplicated and sold to family members. Also do candid videos of parties, promotions, day trips and other special occasions.

29.   Design and manufacture business maternity clothes for businesswomen. Have them stocked in maternity and other women's clothes shops and sell by mail order.

30.   Buy a portable children's mini-railway. Children can sit on the carriages and are taken up and down a short track. Hire out your railway for fund raising at fairs and money-making tourist sites.

31.   Produce 'add-one' plays on audio CDs for amateur actors and actresses. A play is produced and a gap is left in the dialogue for a listener to read the line of a character. A printed copy of the play is provided with each CD.

32.   Design and manufacture kits for making paper at home. Sell the kits to craft workers from ads in crafts magazines and get them stocked in hobby and crafts shops.

33.   Put together a correspondence course about how to write jokes for profit. Base this on a method which is your own invention. For example, jokes are like the keys on a piano: there's a limited number but they can be played in an infinity of combinations.

34.   Open a school for disk jockeys. Offer potential students different courses for radio, night-clubs, mobile discos, hospital radio and pirate radio. Give students tuition: in classes, on a one-to-one basis, or correspondence courses and through audio CDs.

35.   Make low budget promotional videos for pop groups and solo artists who are just starting out. Advertise your service at music shops and in the music press. When you receive an inquiry, give the potential client a persuasive sales presentation.

36.   Bump start your career as a freelance journalist. Newspapers and magazines are always interested in success stories. Find and write about people from humble backgrounds who have been successful in business. The best way to find such people is to advertise for them.

37.   Found an agency for all artists, such as painters, illustrators, pottery workers and sculptors. Provide work for the artists and specialize in contacting businesses which might not have considered using artists. For example, arrange for morals to be painted in staff canteens and sports clubs.

38.   Organize career selection weekends for teenagers. During these weekends teenagers take aptitude tests, receive counseling and listen to talks about various careers.

39.   Bring together a range of products specially designed for left-handed people. Have a catalog printed and start a mail order business.

40.   Build up a sales round where you call on customers once every eight weeks, for example, to sell cheap or unusual household items. First call door-to-door to sell your products then keep a record of buyers and call back eight weeks later to sell other products of a similar nature.

41.   Start a walking menu board service (A sandwich board with a giant menu on it). Sell to restaurants and cafes throughout the region. Employ students and young people to carry the boards.

42.   Write and publish a manual which is about how to start and organize your own football team. Sell from ads in football magazines and programs.

43.   Produce Christmas cards which are printed on the front with, for example, "Happy Christmas from the Smith Family". Or, instead of the name 'Smith', pick one of the dozens of other popular surnames. Sell packs of these cards by direct mail to people listed in telephone directories.

44.   Begin a service which organizes the production of wall hanging tapestries to commission. Sell your service to businesses which might want a tapestry of their logo, for example, hanging

in a reception area. Or do a 1066 style tapestry representing business achievements.

45.   If you can draw amusing caricatures call door-to-door to show people samples of your work and offer to draw one on the spot.

46.   Bring out a selection of baseball caps which are printed with the names of popular sports teams. Distribute to sports shops, gift shops and sell by mail order.

47.   Establish a direct mail business which sells products to pubs, wine bars and hotel bars. The products in your catalog might include: books and booklets about making cocktail drinks, quizzes for contests, promotion ideas, pub games, etc.

48.   Print stationery with a thematic design for hobbyists. For example, photographers can have writing paper and envelopes printed with pictures of cameras, films and lights. Get this stationery stocked at hobby shops and sell by mail order through the appropriate hobby magazines.

49.   Produce a publication which consists entirely of advertisements from sellers of craft-work and craft equipment and supplies. This publication might be like a catalog, but instead of displaying the goods of one seller, it contains ads from hundreds of different sellers.

50.   If you are familiar with electronics, start a mail order business which sells electronic kits, components and accessories. If possible bring out your own electronic kits. To obtain other products get some letterheads printed and write to trade suppliers at home and abroad.

51.   Compile and publish a guide to employers throughout the country who have a high turnover of staff. These employers are always looking for new staff. Sell copies of this guide to job-hunters through bookshops or from classified ads.

52.   Learn how to build garden fences then start your own business. Advertise your garden fence building business in local newspapers and offer to provide a free written estimate.

53.   Begin a postal service which sells the reproduction rights to formulas for making products such as stain removers, special glues and toilet water. Your custom will come from business opportunity seekers who want to reproduce these formulas for reselling. You can also sell the formulas as 'household secrets' through classified ads in women's magazines.

54.   Put together an audio CD course about how to be a successful disc jockey. Sell from ads in music publications and have it stocked in record shops.

55.   Sell flowers at a market or roadside stall.

56.   Begin a woodwork business which makes toys for children which are variations of the traditional rocking horse. For example, rocking mythical creatures, rocking rafts with a single sail, airplanes, UFOs, etc. Sell finished toys or kits through toy shops or by mail order.

57.   Start a mail order business which sells a wide range of dog products, for example: kennels, muzzles, shampoos, collars, ornaments, etc, all with a canine theme.

58.   Invent and design magnetic toys for children or adults. Ideas for toys include: magnetic building blocks, magnetic picture kits, magnetic puzzles, etc. Pay a manufacturer to make the toys. Get your toys stocked by wholesalers, gift shops and toy shops.

59.   If you have the necessary knowledge and skill earn money from teaching home computing in your own home or the home of clients. Prepare lessons on a variety of popular software applications and general computer operation. Give classes and teach to solo students.

60.   Start a venture which promotes the art and hobby of window painting. On colored acetate paper have outlines printed for painting pictures by numbers. These acetate sheets are stuck to one side of a window and anyone can paint a picture on the other side of the glass.

61.   Compose poems to order for any occasion, such as engagements, births, weddings, birthdays, valentines, etc. These poems make a unique and memorable gift. Use classified ads to sell your service. Or set up a stall at a fair or tourist site and compose poems on the spot.

62.   Start a home-based computer bureau. There are hundreds of business computer programs available such as wages, record files and accounts. Buy and use these programs to provide a computer service to local businesses.

63.   Set up a firm which publishes a monthly computer diskette program for home computer enthusiasts who want to improve their program writing skills. Each CD might give ideas, examples and tips about how to become a better computer programmer.

64.   Bring out an audio CD course about how to lose weight. This might employ techniques of self-hypnosis or subliminal suggestion. Sell from ads in slimming and women's magazines.

65.   Set up a dog obedience school. Provide residential courses for owners and their dogs. Also hold courses which teach others to become dog obedience teachers. Advertise in both dog and up-market magazines.

66.   Collect a wide range of aerial photographs. These might be high altitude shots of villages, towns or cities. Start a mail order business which frames and sells these photographs.

67.   Open a school for hostessing. If a woman does hostessing at home she might as well learn to do it properly at your school. Advertise in up-market publications and provide students with a thorough, first class training in being a hostess.

68.   Produce 'Add-One' drama DVDs. Professional actors and actresses perform a play on video. However, there is one character missing from the video. This character is played by a viewer of the video. The viewer learns his or her part and becomes part of the play at home.

69.   Invent and manufacture cosmetics for plants. These should be designed to bring out or emphasize the natural color of plants. Sell you plant cosmetic from ads in gardening magazines or get them displayed by retailers who sell garden products.

70.   Establish a mail order company which sells jokes and tricks. Bring out your own mail order catalog and build up a list of regular customers. Your catalog might specialize in one sector of the market such as women's or X-rated jokes or tricks.

71.   At a tourist site earn money from painting a persons name on a print. The name thus becomes part of the picture. For example, there might be a hoarding of posters in your picture and a persons name becomes one of the posters. Design and produce the prints yourself.

72.   Write and publish a newsletter for those who want to start a crafts business. In each issue give addresses of craft-work buyers. Also include editorial about how to develop both a successful product and a profitable business.

73.   Produce a birthday momento which mock up of a magazine front cover, with the customer's photograph and brief details of the events that took place on that day. Obviously it should be dated when the person was born. It could be printed on large inkjet photo paper and put in a frame.

74.   Begin a board game of the month or quarterly club.

75.   Learn the art of calligraphy. When you become a skilled calligrapher earn money from teaching others in your own home or at evening class.

76.   Turn out knitwear garments for children. Sell the garments from your own stall or through retailers.

77.   Start a mail order business which sells books and products related to the great composers. Conduct a world-wide search for products to include in your catalog Advertise in classical music magazines.

78.   Begin a mail order business which serves those interested in gold prospecting. Sell equipment, supplies and books. Also

publish your own guide to digging for gold in: Wales, USA, Australia, Canada and South America.

79.   Sell recipes for making home-made chocolates and sweets via classified ads. The products made should be of a quality that can be sold either from a stall or to colleagues and friends.

80.   Start a mail order business which sells mosaic making supplies. Also sell a guide about getting started in this hobby. Produce a simple catalog about your products and advertise in crafts magazines.

81.   Bring out a selection of hanging cotton greeting cards. These are like flags or banners which are printed with a greetings message and can be hung from a ceiling or a rail. Arrange for these to be stocked at shops which sell greeting cards.

82.   Bring out a selection of posters which are packed with biblical quotes. Sell these through religious bookshops and by post to schools and practicing Christians.

83.   Start an agency which supplies entertainers to pubs, restaurants and wine bars. The entertainers might include disc jockeys, musicians, singers and strip-tease artists. Visit a lawyer to find what legal requirements you must satisfy. Advertise for entertainers to put on your books, then advertise for business.

84.   Start a crafts business which produces gift tags decorated with pressed flowers. Also do similar products like pressed flowers bookmarks. To make a book-marker tape take two strips of clear 35mm film, place pressed flowers between the strips and tie the sprocket holes together with cotton.

85.   Write and publish a booklet about '101 Ideas for Off The Beaten Track Holidays'. Get this publication stocked at bookshops or sell from classified ads. You might also sell advertising space to firms who organize unusual holidays.

86.   Set up a business which makes wooden dog kennels in kit form. Sell by mail order from ads in dog lovers publications or get them stocked at pets shops.

87.   Buy ordinary plastic model kits of aircraft and boats. Construct the kits and hand paint them in their original colors Sell the finished models from a stall at fairs and markets.

88.   Sell by post information and advice about antiques. Provide clients with a confidential service which identifies and values antiques from descriptions and photographs. Also give advice about care, cleaning and storage of individual items. Produce leaflets about your service.

89.   Open a market stall which specializes in selling tights and stockings.

90.   Produce and distribute an audio CD library of fairy tales. Put together a comprehensive collection of fairy tales. Sell by post as a complete library or start a monthly club. Advertise in women's magazines.

91.   Design and make a selection of gloves for football goalkeepers. Try to add some special feature such as 'extra lightweight', 'extra tough', or 'extra warm'. Have them stocked at sports shops.

92.   Put together a mail order catalog of spoken word audio CDs. Canvass audio CD publishers to see how they can be of help to you. Place as many audio CD titles in this catalog as possible to give potential customers the widest possible choice.

93.   Compile and publish a monthly bulletin which informs subscribers of poetry competitions they are eligible to enter at home and abroad. Target your recruitment campaign for subscribers at practicing poets.

94.   Write and sell articles or books about starting a business and making money. Sell the manuscripts to publishers of business opportunity books, newsletters, magazines and newspapers. For a start, Jon Murray Information Services, 114 Duke Street, Edinburgh, EH6 8HR will welcome any manuscripts for approval and possible purchase.

95.   Design, produce and distribute T-shirts and sweatshirts which have an astronomical theme. The idea is that people will buy a T-shirt or sweat shirt that celebrates their star sign. Package them and have them displayed at a wide range of retailers.

96.   Use the craft of embroidery to make attractive A-Z index cards. Instead of printed cards marked with letters of the alphabet, you make the letters with embroidery. A card index system can now look luxurious. Package the cards and get them stocked at bookshops and stationers.

97.   Make football rosettes and get them stocked at newsagents and sports shops. Each one might be placed in a cellophane packet or polythene bag.

98.   Organize staff suggestion schemes for businesses. Conduct your own research to discover which type of suggestion scheme is the most effective. Then sell your service to businesses.

99.   Make cardboard cut-outs of animals for children. Each cut-out would be six to nine inches high and consist of a photograph or drawing of , for example: an elephant, monkey, tiger or dinosaur. These cut-outs might line a shelf. Package them and sell through shops.

100.   Compile a correspondence course about writing drama or comedy for radio. Radio is a proven route to becoming a successful drama or comedy writer. Your course would help people to develop their writing ability and aid a route into the business.

101.   Run a business which deals in the memorabilia of a region. You can buy your stock from various sources, for example, history books from publishers, photographs from photo libraries and films and videos from film making and film distribution companies.

102.   Produce a rhyming dictionary on audio CDs. A spoken word dictionary can illustrate the rhyming qualities of words far better than any printed dictionary. Get these stocked at bookshops or sell from adverts in literary magazines.

103.   Start a service for newsletter publishers. This might include: handling back issues, enveloping and mailing issues to subscribers, and selling advertising space.

104.   Commission an artist to do a series of designs for saucy postcards. Arrange for the postcards to be printed. Mount the

cards on small racks and distribute these to retailers at tourist resorts.

105.   Write and publish a manual about how to start a profitable antiques market stall. Sell by mail order to opportunity seekers.

106.   Pick a well known old and long road. Research and write the history of that road. Have a few hundred booklets printed and sell to the residents and businesses along the road.

107.   Start a dial-a-gardener service. A single telephone call to you will send a gardener to a customers home. Employ teenagers, students and retired people to do the gardening.

108.   Use logs to make a range of rustic bird tables, nesting compartments and feeders. Have your products stocked at hardware shops and garden centers

109.   Become a wholesaler of spoken word audio CDs. You act as the middleman between publishers and retailers. This is a growth area and it might not be long before every bookshop has many shelves of audio CDs. Will these CDs be supplied by you?!

110.   Design and produce a range of children's badges. These might feature pictures of animals, spacecraft, robots or funny faces. Mount them on a felt covered board or place them in small cellophane packets. Have them displayed at newsagents and toy shops

111.   Start a collectable plate of the month club. Commission the making of attractive plates and slowly build up a list of club members.

112.   Begin a service which produces newsletters for pop group fan clubs. Devise a method for producing a reasonable newsletter at low cost. Sell your service to fan clubs. An important part of this business is that it gives a lot of scope for the selling of advertising space.

113.   Begin a business which specializes in organizing romantic breaks and holidays. Arrange for courting couples, newly-weds and mature couples to have breaks at hunting lodges, cottages and castles.

114.   Establish a marketplace for computer hardware. On a computer or card index system list details of what sellers have to sell. Charge the sellers a fee. Place ads in computer magazines which invite telephone inquiries from people looking for computer hardware.

115.   Start a mail order business which sells started kits for being an amateur musician. Put the kits together from products which are already on the market.

116.   Buy old bibles and hymn books from churches and education authorities. Have the pages shredded and use as stuffing material for 'bible' or 'hymn' pillows, teddy bear and other soft products. Also do 'bible' confetti and stuff bottles to make bottled bibles.

117.   Start a business which sells custom designed drinks bars from home. Operate this business in a similar style to firms which sell fitted wardrobes or kitchens.

118.   Begin a mail order business which sells football videos, photographs, postcards, posters and slides. Advertise in football magazines and programs.

119.   Start a miniature brass-ware ornament of the month club. Or produce a mail order catalog which has a very wide range of brass ornaments.

120.   Begin a firm which produces and distributes a range of I'm in love' products. These will include T-shirts, car stickers and badges.

121.   Package individual apples, oranges and bananas. Sell through newsagents and other suitable shops.

122.   Learn about flower arranging at evening classes then, earn money from teaching others in your own home. Give afternoon classes to pensioners and housewives. A major attraction of the classes is that they act as a social occasion.

123.   Write and produce an audio CD course for those who want to stop smoking. Sell this course through adverts in newspapers and magazines or by direct mail to business people.

124.   Make charming and attractive quilts for babies and children. Make the kind of quilts you would like a baby or child to have. Give your imagination free reign to see what ideas and designs you come up with. When you have finalized a design, go into business for yourself.

125.   Start a mail order catalog which specializes in products which aid abstinence. For example, products for giving up: Smoking, Swearing, Nail Biting, Drinking, etc.

126.   Manufacture wooden TV caddies for holding an ashtray, drink, sandwiches, TV programs schedule, Kleenex, etc. A TV caddie might consist of an upright plank of wood with several shelves.

127.   Start a service which produces high quality, demonstration audio CDs for new pop groups. The groups pay for the production of the CDs. Your service also distributes copies to people in the music business. Advertise in the music press.

128.   Start a mobile installation and repair service for all kinds of car lights. Produce a leaflet which lists prices for different jobs. Deliver the leaflets to houses or stick behind windscreen wipers of cars in your area.

129.   Set up a firm which hires out sunbeds. Use local advertising to publicize your service and offer clients a free delivery service.

130.   Devise unique cocktail drinks and punches to commission. Name each drink after the person nominated by the sponsor. These recipes make unusual gifts, for example, a specially designed punch would add fun to a wedding reception or birthday. Sell from classified ads.

131.   Start a thimble of the month club for new and established thimble collectors. Members of the club receive the club's choice of thimble of the month.

132.   Devise role-playing games which can be played by post. For example, someone has to plan an expedition or business venture and he or she receives feedback by post. Set up a postal

role-playing games club and charge members a fee for each game they participate in.

133.   Devise and produce an audio CD course about successful exam techniques. An important selling point is that anyone with average intelligence can pass most exams if they know about exam techniques.

134.   Learn the art of making stained glass windows. Use your newly acquired skills to earn money from: 1) Teaching people in your own home, 2) Holding courses at bed and breakfast houses out of season, 3) holding classes in a quiet corner or back room of an arts and crafts shop.

135.   Start a service which makes audio tape recordings of wedding ceremonies. video cameras are either not allowed in church or produce poor pictures. However, discreet microphones can record the ceremony. Copies on CD can be sent to friends and relatives at home and overseas.

136.   Buy and sell second hand household goods from local newspaper adverts.

137.   Produce a cataloging system for record collectors. This system might consist of a card index box with pre-printed index cards. Each card has a printed section for the name of the artist, record and record label. Sell this cataloging system through record shops or by mail-order.

138.   Open a school of computing. Rent an office and teach or employ others to teach courses about computing. The most financially rewarding courses would be those which help students to get jobs in computing.

139.   Use ball bearings to make attractive ornaments, either 1) decorate large ball bearings or 2) stick smaller ball bearings together. The ornaments might be shaped to look like people or animals. Sell through gift shops or from a stall.

140.   Produce and distribute a video encyclopedia about flowers, plants, trees or birds. This should present DVDs about your chosen subject in alphabetical order. Try to get national and international distribution organized.

141.   Produce painting by numbers outlines specially designed for hobbyists. For example, do outlines of locomotives, or background scenery for railway modelers. Sell these from ads in hobby magazines or get them stocked at modeling shops.

142.   Produce T-shirts which are printed with the names of local schools. Have them stocked at newsagents or other suitable shops close to each school.

143.   Write and publish a newsletter which deals with most aspects of self-improvement. The newsletter might consist of ideas for getting ahead and mini courses about self-improvement. Sell subscriptions internationally.

144.   Write and publish a newsletter which is about how to sell simple information by post. In each newsletter suggest new ideas for the kind of information which can be sold. Also review the latest offerings by other information sellers.

145.   Start a business which produces periscopes for viewing things underwater. For example, at the seaside, or at a lake, a person on the surface can put the periscope into the water and look around underwater.

146.   Publish a newsletter about human interest stories, unusual facts, interesting paragraphs, etc. Subscribers would include people who produce their own, regular, amateur publication. They would use your newsletter as a source to provide fillers for their own publication.

147.   Learn machine knitting. Once your skill has reached a high standard, earn money from teaching others to use knitting machines. Teach people in your own home or theirs.

148.   Design and manufacture kits for making models with cocktail sticks, for example: model churches, castles, windmills, houses, etc. Buy the cocktail sticks in their unpacked state from the manufacturer. Sell your kits by mail order from ads in craft magazines or distribute to model shops.

149.   Be a success consultant. Earn an income from giving advice on how people can achieve success. Start by reaching a clear definition of what a client means by success. Do an assessment of clients strengths and weaknesses and suggest, for example, a program of changes in approach and career.

150.   Open a press cutting research service for stock market investors. Read the daily papers and make a note every time a public company is mentioned. When an investor requests information about a company, you photocopy all the cuttings which mention the name of that company.

151.   Sell by post to record collectors unsorted parcels of new and second-hand records. Less than 5% of singles released get into the top 20 of the charts. So there are a lot of new unsold singles in the hands of record companies.

152.   Use leather to make key-ring fobs. Burn designs or put studs into the fobs and add a key-ring. Sell from a stall or find suitable retail outlets.

153.   Publish poetry in a way similar to music sheets. On a printed folded sheet feature a main poem and maybe 3 or 4 support poems. Get these 'poem sheets' stocked at bookshops and newsagents. The price might be the same as a daily newspaper. Also organize a chart of top selling poem sheets.

154.   If you have the artistic ability to sketch or do ink drawings of private houses there is certainly money to be made here. get work by calling on households in the nicer looking parts of town and showing potential customers samples of your work. Also offer a framing service.

155.   Devise and produce an audio CD course about how to play the drums. Use ads in the music press to sell this course. And/or get the course stocked at music shops.

156.   Produce a selection of memory adoption CDs. People often wish they had more pleasant childhood memories than they do. These CDs would consist of recordings of pleasant memories. A listener can adopt these memories and pretend they are his or her own.

157.   Launch a carved ornament of the month club. A collection of beautifully carved ornaments will add character to a house and make a good investment.

158.   Set up a marriage bureau in your area. Provide your clients with a personal, sincere and caring service which searches for suitable life partners.

159.   Start a venture which organizes river or coastal boat trips for: Business parties, wedding receptions, anniversaries, birthday parties, etc. Your service would do things like: organize transport to the boat, booking catering services, hiring entertainers and hosts or hostesses.

160.   Put together a kit for growing trees from seeds. In each kit include instructions about how to get the best results. Sell from ads in gardening publications or through suitable shops.

161.   Buy fantasy role-playing games from those who make up games as a hobby. Publish the games in a monthly newsletter and sell subscriptions to fantasy role-playing enthusiasts throughout the country.

162.   Conduct your own research into the subject of how to make money from gaming machines. Write and publish a report about your findings. Sell from classified ads or by direct mail and emphasize that people could make a lot of money from buying your report.

163.   Make Punch and Judy soft toys or dolls. Sell these toys and dolls through seaside shops. Or get Punch and Judy performers to sell them to patrons.

164.   Give tuition to those who want to enlarge their vocabulary. Your advertising material might include a word test similar to Reader's Digest's 'Test Your Word power' and an offer to improve the score.

165.   Earn money by selling all sorts of formulas by post. For example: formulas to DIY enthusiasts, housewives, hobbyists, craft-workers and many others. Produce either a general directory

which has universal appeal or bring out specialize booklets for different markets.

166.   Start a mail order business which specializes in selling classic singles from the sixties. Classic singles are constantly being re-issued in various countries around the world. Import these and sell by post.

167.   Make a selection of saucy 'warmers' such as nipple warmers, belly-button warmers, bum warmers, willy warmers, etc. Put each warmer into a plastic bag, staple a card naming the product to each bag. Find shops to stock them.

168.   Design and manufacture kits for making clothes. The kits might be aimed at those who have basic sewing skills, but would need a kit if they want to make something a bit more complex. Produce a catalog about your kits and advertise in women's magazines.

169.   Develop your dog grooming skills to a professional standard and open your own dog grooming parlor.

170.   Make kitchen wall-pouches from either leather or fabrics. Each pouch is for holding money-off coupons, shopping lists and other bits of paper which are worth keeping. Find retailers to stock your wall-pouches.

171.   Produce booklets or audio CDs which contain gay short stories. sell by mail order or have them stocked in shops which are used by the gay community.

172.   Begin a mail order business which sells exposes. Produce booklets, audio CDs and information sheets about, for example:

wealthy left-wing politicians, worthless aristocrats, stonewall secret service bungling, bureaucratic incompetence, violent police, etc.

173.   Start a newsletter for people who want to make money from their home computer. In each issue provide subscribers with ideas for adventure games, educational or quiz programs, and business programs. Also print news, tips and case studies about starting a computing business.

174.   Create a mail order business which specializes in selling products which help people sleep. Products might include: Sleep inducing CDs, special bedtime clothing, herbal pillows, books and guides on how to sleep better.

175.   Start a children's telephone pal club. Pen pal clubs help children develop their writing ability, this club helps them to become accustomed to using the telephone. Each member receives introductory notes about the interests of the child he or she will shortly speak to.

176.   Be a family relations consultant. Give advice about how to improve relationships with family members. If you can provide a satisfactory standard of advice your local area should provide you with enough business.

177.   Design and make novelty soft toys and caps. For example, a soft toy sledgehammer is attached to a cap so that it looks like it is embedded. Also make hats with antennae and horns.

178.   Set up a garden improvement business which designs and builds ornamental Japanese or Chinese gardens. Produce a

brochure about your work and advertise in up-market publications.

179.   Produce magnetic perpetual calendars. A strip of metal is printed with day numbers and the names of months. Two magnetic markers are used to indicate the date.

180.   Advertise for job lots in local and national publications. See what offers turn up and buy anything you think you can resell for a profit.

181.   Produce framed prints of pin-ups. These might be X-rated for sale by mail order, classic pin-ups of the 40s, 50s and 60s or contemporary pin-ups.

182.   Begin a business which organizes short courses and seminars for salespeople. A guest successful sales personality might be selected to give each lesson. The subjects you cover might include: 'How to Double Your Sales' and 'How to Beat Your Competitors'.

183.   Rent out model trains by post to railway enthusiasts. This service would allow enthusiasts to examine and use a wide range of trains. You could include an option for the customer to buy if they are particularly fond of any model.

184.   Make household hall letter boards A board is criss-crossed with colored elastic. Letters are slipped behind this elastic and thus easily displayed. Have them stocked at stationers and gift shops. Or sell by mail order.

185.   Bring together a range of brass-ware ornaments so you can have a stall at crafts fairs, antique markets and car boot sales.

186.   Be a home visiting wig salesperson. By visiting the homes of potential buyers you provide a private and confidential service which is free of embarrassment. Buy a selection from wig manufacturers at trade prices. Advertise your service in newspapers and magazines.

187.   Organize weekend breaks where people can experience 'living' history. Guests can spend a weekend living in a re-created era of history such as the Stone Age, the Wild West or Viking times.

188.   Set up a party plan business which sells gardening equipment and supplies. You might, for example, hold the parties in gardens during the afternoons. Once you have developed a successful presentation and range of products, increase the size of your business by recruiting agents.

189.   Produce and distribute a video encyclopedia. A video encyclopedia consists of a series of film clips with very little description. All the film clips might relate to one subject such as cars, trains, ships, or airplanes. The clips might appear in alphabetical or chronological order.

190.   Set up a school of 'Self-selling'. Teach students at your school how to sell themselves and impress, for example: The opposite sex, work colleagues, job interviewers, etc. Hold classes, give individual tuition, or teach people through audio CDs or correspondence courses.

191.   Each month produce and interesting lecture on audio CD. Sell these through a monthly club. The subjects should be something which appeals to an established market such as science fiction fans, business opportunity seekers or sales people.

192.   Start a manufacturing business which is devoted to making doorstops. These doorstops might range from the humble wooden wedge to the more exotic and unusual. Package them in polythene bags, staple on a printed card and get them stocked at gift shops.

193.   Bring together a selection of products related to chess. For example: books, ornaments, framed prints, chess playing accessories, etc. Produce a catalog and sell by mail order.

194.   Start an enterprise which organizes arts and crafts fairs. Find suitable venues, rent spaces to artists and craft-workers. Publicize throughout the local area.

195.   Launch a rose of the month club. Build up a list of clients who want a rose sent each month to their loved one.

196.   Set up a business which produces a quality audio CD library of nursery rhymes. Alternatively, produce a series of CDs which feature X-rated nursery rhymes for adults. Sell these by either getting them stocked in bookshops or by starting a monthly club.

197.   Start a home party hire service. The hosts of children's and adults' parties hire from you: chairs, tables, cutlery, plates, glasses, barbecues, etc. Advertise your service either in local newspapers or newsagents windows. Provide a free delivery service.

198.   Organize weekend courses for DIY enthusiasts. Provide students with practical tuition about various popular DIY projects. Advertise in DIY magazines.

199.   Invent ideas for practical jokes. Sell these by either producing a regular newsletter or, a directory of jokes for different occasions. You might also set up a national practical jokes club.

200.   Place advertisements in the windows of local newsagents which read 'Lawn cutting done' and state an hourly rate. When you visit customers, offer to cut their lawn on a regular basis.

201.   Set up a business which produces cinema programs. These programs might consist of 2-8 printed pages. Sell advertising space in these programs to local businesses and include details of future films. Cinema programs take these programs from a display unit free of charge.

202.   Bring out a series of booklets or CDs which have titles like : 'How to Cure Boredom', 'How to Beat Depression', 'How to Get Out of a Rut', 'How to Beat Back Pain', etc. Sell by mail order, through bookshops or other retail outlets.

203.   Form a mail order business which sells unusual plants. For example: insect eating plants. Conduct your own search for a suitable plant. Every now and again someone discovers a new, unusual plant for selling by post an makes a fair amount of money. Will you be next?

204.   Earn a living by buying gold and silver jewelery from people who need instant cash. Because their need for cash is greater than their desire to get a high price, your mark-up can be good. Only buy jewelery which you know you can re-sell quickly for a profit.

205.   Begin a gift service which provides a nostalgic selection of magazines from the month of a person's birth. Advertise your service in the columns or classified ads which feature other gift ideas.

206.   Produce personalized place mats for toddlers. It comprises of a picture of a knife, fork and plate with the child's favorite character or animal on it, with the child's name on it. Have it printed on card or thick paper and laminated.

207.   At a public place or fair have a site where people can pay to do their own action painting. Each person is given overalls and a canvass or large sheet of paper. They can then help themselves to as much paint as they like and all kinds of brushes and implements.

208.   Start a weekly car cleaning and polishing service. Build up a list of clients by calling on households in your area to promote the service. Employ teenagers, students and fit retired people to do the cleaning and polishing.

209.   Set up a service which organizes holiday exchanges between people who live in English speaking countries and those in Japan and Continental Europe.

210.   Design your own brand of baby sling. Buy one of each of the baby slings currently on sale. Study them and develop one which is a composite of the best features. Manufacture and package them. Find appropriate retailers and wholesalers to stock them.

211.   Learn the craft of woodcarving. When you become skilled earn money from carving popular first names in relief and turn

these into brooches. Also turn out other carved jewelery such as pendants, bracelets and earrings.

212.   Begin a service which helps car owners to sell their cars. You would have around twenty sites at newsagents, barbers, supermarkets, etc, where details of the cars are displayed. A car owner pays you, for example, £20, half goes to you and half to the site owners.

213.   Put together a home study course about theatrical directing. Call this business a postal drama school. Students will include: amateur drama directors, professional actors and other theater enthusiasts.

214.   Write and record personalized songs. Produce songs for all occasions, such as engagements, weddings, birthdays, anniversaries, births, homecomings and congratulations. Use classified ads in the personal columns to attract orders.

215.   Sell pegs, dishcloths and dusters door-to-door. All you need to do is to buy these goods from a wholesaler, place them in a shopping basket and you are in business.

216.   Set up a mail order business which sells books and products related to ventriloquism. Produce booklets and CDs which give instructions about ventriloquism and ideas for stage acts. Also sell props and dummies.

217.   Bring out a cataloging system for book buyers to use at home. For example, have a card index with pre-printed cards. The cards have printed on them: spaces for the name of the author, the book title, etc. Also include self-adhesive numbers. Sell your card index system through bookshops.

218.   Write and publish a newsletter which is specifically for budding and practicing freelance writers. Give the newsletter a title like: 'Freelance Writer'. Give ideas and tips about how to sell work and have a section for articles, letters and classified ads.

219.   Start a trade publication for small mail order businesses. Give the latest news and views relevant to small mail order businesses. Distribute by post.

220.   Start a mail order business which sells books, equipment and supplies to those interested in amateur rocketry. Put together an amateur rocketry kit for beginners and advertise this to attract new hobbyists to the business.

221.   Organize overseas information gathering tours for businesspeople. These might be for those who want to look at an overseas market or who want to visit similar businesses to their own in other countries. For example, consultants in this country can visit their foreign counterparts.

222.   Create a correspondence course about how to be more enterprising. Sell by placing ads in national newspapers. Have ad headlines like: 'Are you an enterprising person?', and 'Improve your life by being more enterprising'.

223.   Bring out a book or audio CD which has a title like: 'How to get a World Record'. Include information about how to get a record accepted and give ideas about feats which might be attempted. Sell through bookshops or by post.

224.   Bring out a series of audio CDs or booklets which give advice about how to deal with the problems experienced by teenagers. For example: the search for identity and career choices.

Aim style and contents at either the teenagers themselves or at parents.

225. Begin a mail order business which sells books and study equipment to those interested in natural history.

226. Build elaborate sand-castles or sand sculptures at the seaside and accept donations from those who want to show appreciation of your work.

227. Publish a newsletter which has the title "Ambitious Persons Way to Wealth" or "Clever People Don't Work Hard". The contents of your newsletter might be in a vein similar to Joe Karbo's "The Lazy Man's Way to Riches".

228. Produce a series of booklets about how to buy and run various types of shops. Each booklet might cover a shop such as a newsagent, greengrocer, village shop, post office, etc. Place classified ads in newspapers and magazines which advertise shops for sale and sell your booklets by mail.

229. Start a private school for florists. Provide courses for those who want to either set up in business or want to get a job as a florist. Advertise in women's magazines.

230. Publish a 'Who's Who of Business Opportunities'. Sell advertising space in this publication to business opportunity firms. Use direct mail and ads in the business opportunity press to sell advertising space and the finished publication.

231. Set up a caddie service for photographers, film makers and video makers. Hire out yourself, and others, to carry equipment for people in these groups. Place ads in suitable magazines to

offer your service and send a leaflet to photographers who do location work for businesses.

232.   Bring out a selection of lucky charms which are for hanging from windscreens of cars, vans and lorries. They might be mini horse shoes, rabbits feet, wooden or plastic number sevens, four-leaf clovers, etc. Package your lucky charms to distribute to a wide range of retailers.

233.   Produce novelty car stickers which feature a big 'X' stamped across pictures of traffic wardens, policemen, or cars. They are designed to be stuck to cars in the fashion of fighter planes to show enemy airplanes destroyed. They are for amusement only and should appeal to a wide range of drivers.

234.   Bring out a correspondence course or audio CD course, about how to write good dialogue for fiction. Sell through ads in publications for writers.

235.   Open a small private school of art. Employ artists to teach courses about different kinds of art from oil painting to pottery. Offer holiday courses, individual tuition and evening and weekend classes.

236.   Design and manufacture finger painting kits for children and adults. Get these stocked at shops which sell toys (for children's kits) and artists materials (for adult's kits).

237.   During the Christmas season, form a group of carol singers. Hire this group out to parties, restaurants, wine bars, and night-clubs.

238.	Bring out an 'ideas' newsletter for writers. In each issue suggest ideas for: locations, characters, events, phrases, use of words, etc. One of the main selling points of your newsletter is that it will help a writer to become a published author.

239.	Bring out a correspondence course about how to write cookery books. The course might include information about: How to devise recipes, how to present them in written form and what makes a successful cookery book. Produce a prospectus and advertise in women's magazines.

240.	Devise your own brand of Bombay mix snack. Set up a business which makes and packages the snack. Sell through newsagents and grocers.

241.	Buy and sell oil paintings. Buy new paintings from artists and old paintings from collectors and householders. Sell the paintings from: home, a roadside site, a stall at crafts fairs or hire stalls for exhibiting all the paintings you have for sale.

242.	Hire a hall at a city center location - Saturday would be the best day - and sell women's clothes at low prices.

243.	Introduce to your region a service which mounts maps for businesses. Keep a stock of local, national and international maps. Mount these maps in a professional manner to suit the wall space available at offices. Send out leaflets about your services to office managers.

244.	Make money from renting out expensive children's toys. The toys you rent out will include remote controlled models and computerized games. Use a little van to deliver the toys to customers. Paint in toy town color scheme. Call the van a toy mobile or similar suitable name.

245.   Found a stop smoking club. Hold club meetings at hired halls in various areas on different nights of the week. Employ a variety of techniques to help people to give up smoking. A great many people will be driven by the collective inspiration of the group.

246.   Design, produce and distribute your own brand of anti-smoking ashtray. For example, produce an ashtray which is either, a model of a cancerous lung or printed with the names of people who died on the same day from lung cancer.

247.   Make wooden badges in the shape of teddy bears, pigs, elephants, etc. Use a fret saw to cut the shapes and add a few strokes of paint to bring the shapes to life. Mount these badges on a board covered with a fabric. Ask shopkeepers to display one of the badge covered boards.

248.   Put together a mail order catalog which has a wide range of business posters. The posters might be about: inspiring, sales efficiency, hard work and saving energy. Send the catalog to most businesses.

249.   Publish a newsletter about the changing English language. The contents would provide information about new words and meanings. Sell subscriptions to writers, academics, advertising agencies and others who might be interested in new words.

250.   Set up a mail order business which sells casting equipment, supplies and books. Potential customers include a wide range of craft-workers and hobbyists. Begin by learning

everything you can about small scale casting then track down trade suppliers of products related to casting.

251.   Carve wooden ornaments which look like gargoyles. Attach to one side of the ornament a sticky baked material or magnet. They can then be added to car dashboards or to fridges.

252.   Set up and organize a home-visiting massage service. Your business would find work for experienced masseurs and masseuses. Get custom by placing ads in local newspapers and notices in the windows of local newsagents.

253.   Start a business which imports folk music instruments. Many overseas folk music instruments are made by individuals or small firms who have not considered selling their products in this country. Distribute the imported folk instruments to music shops or sell by mail order.

254.   Cut out prints and illustrations from old books. Frame them and sell to a wide range of shops and from a stall at a market fairs and car boot sales.

255.   Design garden ornaments which create special effects on mid-summer's day. Start a business which builds and sells your designs. You might, for example, advertise in occult publications.

256.   Begin a mail order business which sells folk crafts. Pick a national group such as the Scots, Welsh or Irish. Put together hampers and folk craft products which capture the essence of your chosen group. Have a catalog printed and advertise it around the world.

257.   Establish a one-man, dial-a-handyman service. Produce a leaflet which lists examples of the jobs you do and your prices. Deliver leaflets to households and businesses in your area. Use a telephone answering machine to take calls while you are out.

258.   Earn from illustrating personal names in the style of Dickens' illustrator George Cruikshank. Do work at: tourist sites, shopping thoroughfares, fairs, exhibitions, etc. Also do illustrations by post and offer a service which reproduces your work on personal stationery.

259.   Bring out a selection of musical book-markers. To make the book-markers musical use electronic devices similar to the ones used in musical greeting cards.

260.   Earn from selling flowers door-to-door. Buy stock from a flower wholesaler or market. Build up a regular base of clients who you can expect to buy a bunch every week from you.

261.   Design and make a selection of baby christening outfits. Sell the outfits by mail order or through shops which sell children's clothes.

262.   Produce and launch a correspondence course which teaches people how to write fiction for adolescents for profit.

263.   Bring out a correspondence course about how to write short stories for profit. Sell from newspaper and magazine ads and charge anything up to the average weekly wage (paid in installments) depending on the contents of the course.

264.   Start a firm which designs and manufactures noticeboards for the home and office. These might have a special feature, for

example, cover the boards with a fabric which has an exotic design or make boards which have an unusual shape.

265.   Set up a mail order business which is devoted to selling products designed to increase a persons attractiveness to the opposite sex. Products might include books, CDs, courses, systems and aids. Produce some of the products yourself.

266.   Sell by post plans for hobby electronic construction projects. Buy plans from established electronics hobbyists and compile a catalog of plans for sale. Find and sell plans through adverts in electronic hobby magazines.

267.   Start a computerized horse-racing results prediction service. There are many systems available for selecting a winning horse. Base your computer program on any or a mixture of these systems. Send forecasts on a regular basis to subscribers.

268.   Familiarize yourself with products on sale at shops which sell arts and crafts materials. Visit similar shops abroad to find a good product or products that are not on sale in this country. Start a business importing and distributing your chosen product.

269.   Bring together a selection of books and CDs about self-hypnosis and start a mail order business. Produce a catalog about your products and send it to those interested in astrology, the occult and self-improvement.

270.   Reprint classic photographs and set up a mail order business to sell these reprints to amateur and professional photographers.

271.   Put together a debt collection training course for small businesses. Every small business is a potential client. A key selling point is that the cost of the course should be quickly recovered from the more efficient collection of debts.

272.   Set up a sheet music of the month club. Each month send members a selection of sheets to include the latest popular songs. Club members will include: Musicians, who play at clubs and pubs, record companies and keen amateur musicians.

273.   Produce cardboard, sightseeing periscopes and sell them at public events. Make them yourself. Arrange for the card to be printed and shaped. Assemble the periscopes and add two small mirrors. Recruit sales people to sell these periscopes along the route of the event.

274.   Set up your own furniture removals business. Start by hiring a van to do the removals and if business proves promising, buy your own van.

275.   Organize courses for those who would like to start their own crafts business. Offer students specialized courses about starting a soft-toy, for example, or pottery business. Hold courses at either crafts workshops or bed and breakfast houses during the off-season time.

276.   Start an enterprise which makes airport type wind-socks in miniature for ordinary gardens. Distribute these to hardware shops and garden centers or sell by mail order from ads in gardening publications.

277.   Make kites which feature Union Jacks, Stars and Stripes or the colors of popular football teams. Package and have stocked at suitable retailers.

278.   Begin a business which organizes trips to rock and pop concerts, and football and rugby matches. Your service obtains the tickets and provides a coach or mini-bus to take fans to the venue.

279.   Make peg calendars. A peg calendar consists of a block of wood with a line of 31 holes for days, 12 holes for months, and 10 holes for years. Three tiny pegs indicate the date and are moved each day accordingly. The calendar can hang from a wall like a thermometer or sit on a desk.

280.   Contact the owners of houses with small letterboxes and offer to supply and install a large letterbox.

281.   Produce a correspondence course about how to write good poetry. If most poets received a small amount of tuition about how to compose poems, their work would improve dramatically. Sell the course by advertising in literary and women's magazines.

282.   Make novel paperweights by modifying: snooker balls, golf balls, cricket balls, pool balls, etc. Get them stocked at stationers, sports clubs and gift shops.

283.   Write and publish a manual which has a title like 'How to Start Your Own Mail Order Business'. Use classified ads and direct mail to sell this to business opportunity seekers.

284.   Start a service which specializes in removing and applying wallpaper. Produce a leaflet which both describes your first class

service and lists your prices. Deliver leaflets to households in your area or advertise in the local paper.

285.   Recreate classic chess games on video. Start a business which hires and sells these to chess enthusiasts.

286.   Cut divining rods for selling by mail order to gardeners and curiosity seekers. A divining rod would also make an interesting and unusual gift.

287.   Be a sleep consultant. Large numbers of people have difficulty in sleeping at night. This is not usually a medical problem but can be corrected by using a suitable method or attitude of mind. Provide people in your area with confidential advice about how to sleep soundly.

288.   Package pressed flowers. Each packet might contain an individual set, or unsorted selection, of pressed flowers. Attach the packets to display cards, or place in a display box and distribute to arts and crafts shops.

289.   Start an enterprise which makes a high quality, home-made paper. Sell the paper at a premium for use as : Personal stationery, certificate presentation scrolls, printing paper for manually operated printing presses, etc.

290.   Commission artists to do original paintings of horses and horse racing. Set up a business which distributes and sells these paintings. For example your might display the paintings in a mobile showroom which visits horse events.

291.   Produce biographical photographs of celebrities. For example, read all about the Beatles or the Rolling Stones to

discover : Their places of birth, schools, first places of work, houses they once lived in, etc. Take photographs of these places, and put dates of birth below portrait photographs and sell to fans.

292.   Make a selection of children's prayer plaques: Wooden wall plates which feature popular prayers. The prayers might be painted onto or burned into the wood.

293.   begin a computerized dating service. Operate this service like a traditional dating service but, hold all your records on computer and use the computer to aid your search for compatible partners. Have leaflets printed and place them in shops and advertise your service in the personal messages section of your local newspapers.

294.   Use small sea-shells strung together to make necklaces. Find a trade source of small sea-shells and either set up your own production line or employ homeworkers.

295.   Put together a correspondence course which teaches people how to play bridge. Call your business a school of bridge. Advertise in up-market publications.

296.   Design and make original fashion clothes. Begin by selling your work from a market stall. This will give you the valuable experience of meeting fashion buyers face-to-face. If you discover you can make clothes which are popular, branch out and sell to boutiques.

297.   Sell Beatles or Elvis memorabilia by mail order. Conduct your own research to discover what memorabilia you can produce yourself, for example, reprint photographs and duplicate

press cuttings. Also buy goods from collectors and trade sources at home and abroad.

298.   Start a market stall which sells low valued antiques. Obtain stock from either trade sources or buy salable goods from the public.

299.   Learn how to catch and eradicate rodents. When your skill reaches a high standard, go into business for yourself. Get a listing for your services in the Yellow Pages.

300.   Prepare a mixture of dried herbs for adding to bathwater. Invent a brand name for your product like "(your surname) Original Bath Herbs". Package each mixture of herbs and get them stocked at various retailers.

301.   Bring out a regular publication for ambitious amateur musicians. This publication might include ads from : 1) Employers seeking musicians. 2) Retailers selling equipment accessories and supplies. 3) People selling used equipment. 4) Musicians seeking to make contact with other musicians. Also publish interesting editorials and letters.

302.   Start a life history photography service. Produce an album of photographs which is a photographic history of a client's life. For example take photographs of a client's hospital of birth, former schools, places of work, place of marriage, houses they once lived in, etc.

303.   Start a firm which manufacturers kits for making etchings. Design the kits so that a complete beginners can make attractive etchings. Sell by mail order or through shops which sell artists' materials.

304.   Start a service which buries personalized time capsules which contain items of a persons choice. Advertise your service in up-market publications. Or start a mail order service which sells time capsules to people who want to bury things on their property.

305.   Make cotton gloves especially designed for coin collectors. The gloves prevent the grease and moisture from fingers getting onto coins. Package the gloves and sell them from ads in coin collecting magazines or distribute to shops which sell collectible coins.

306.   Become a magician for birthday, school and office parties. If you can do magic tricks which most people haven't seen before then you could be a big hit.

307.   Organize educational holidays and weekend breaks for computer enthusiasts who want to further their programming skills. The courses might be held at a bed and breakfast house out of season. Advertise in computing magazines.

308.   Set up a home-improvement business which modifies the exterior of houses to give them a Tudor appearance. Your service will include the fitting of ornamental oak beams, giving exterior walls a white covering and adding metal grids to windows.

309.   Produce a series of storytelling videos. An actor or actress reads classic novels directly to the camera. Hire out these videos by post. You can use whole or part of classic stories for which the copyright has expired. This is the case for any work where the writer has been dead for 50 or more years.

310.   Publish a "Which?" newsletter about newsletters. As the number of newsletters and subscribers is ever increasing, there is a gap in the market for a newsletter which comments on and judges the value of the others.

311.   Bring out a selection of hair jewelery. This could be made from real or artificial human hair and is knotted like dreadlocks. The jewelery also includes colored beads in the design. The result is dreadlocks necklaces, brooches and earrings.

312.   Begin a club which sends philatelists a set of stamps every month. The sets might be either, thematic or newly issued by a country chosen by the collector.

313.   Write and publish a series of booklets or CDs about how to make money from flowers and plants. The titles might include: 'Starting a Florists', 'Setting up a Nursery', and 'How to Open a Garden Center'. Advertise in gardening magazines.

314.   Create a company which designs and manufactures children's kits for : making kaleidoscopes, constructing pinhole cameras, growing crystals, and other things which demonstrate simple scientific principles. You might include all the projects in a compendium of basic scientific experiments.

315.   Prepare a correspondence course about how to increase chances at winning at poker, the pools or horse-racing. The course allows people to develop their skills over a period of time and allows you to charge a reasonable amount of money. Use press advertising to sell.

316.   Produce souvenir children's height charts which feature postcard-type views of local scenery. Or do souvenir suntan

charts. These suntan charts have a complete range of skin shades. A holiday-maker buys a suntan chart to make a before and after comparison.

317.   Add a stand to fragments of original rock from Mount Everest and sell through gift shops or ads in mountaineering publications. You might also do the same for other major mountains.

318.   Make money from wines by taking an empty van to a wine growing region and bringing it back full. Sell the wine directly to restaurants, off-licenses, and free houses. Build up a list of business who will buy wine from you on a regular basis.

319.   Become a street handbag polisher. This service is similar to a street shoeshine, except handbags are polished. Also offer to polish leather clothes, such as jackets and coats.

320.   Write and publish a newsletter for those who want to make money with their photographic or video camera. In each issue give a detailed description of a selected enterprise. Also provide subscribers with other money making ideas and news and tips about photography and video making.

321.   Open a market stall which sells celebrity products. Sell books, badges, posters and other products on the latest celebrities. These celebrities will include new pop stars, film stars, models and national heroes. Also sell products about classic celebrities like the Beatles and Elvis.

322.   Assemble sets of fossils. These might be based on a type of animal, for example, insects or fish. Or organize them according to particular geological periods. Sell to collectors and schools.

323.   Produce a series of biographical audio CDs about well-known businesspeople. Bring out a catalog and send it to business and professional people. Or start a monthly club where a subscriber receives a different CD every month.

324.   Set up a business which makes nightshirts and nightcaps. Have these stocked at up-market clothes retailers.

325.   Introduce to your area a daily home-visiting, morning make-up service. Build up a timetable of appointments with different clients. Or work for a local hotel providing a make-up service for the guests.

326.   Start a service which arranges for people to have their original pop lyrics set to music. This service is to satisfy the vanity of lyricists. Offer clients a complete, low cost package. Attract custom by placing ads in the music press.

327.   Introduce a service to your area which releases lighter than air balloons at weddings, birthdays and other special occasions. Buy a cylinder of gas and turn out the balloons yourself. Offer potential clients a selection of quantities for different prices.

328.   Design a selection of bookplates. They might have a theme related to, for example: Greek gods, astrology, rural scenery, trains, etc. Have them printed and packaged in cellophane packets. Sell through bookshops and stationers.

329.   Produce prints of horses and horse racing. These might be reproduced in a catalog and sold by direct mail to horse lovers. Also offer trade discounts for quantities of prints.

330. Start a modern art rental business. Rent out everything from metal sculptures to mobile art. Your potential clients will include all image conscious businesses with reception areas, courtyards or forecourts.

331. If you have advanced knowledge of mathematics or computing, make an income from devising mathematical or computing puzzles. Sell these to magazines, newspapers and book publishers.

332. Make military play uniforms for children. For example: 7th Cavalry, navy uniforms, toy soldier uniforms, etc. Package and sell through toy shops. Alternatively have a catalog produced and sell by mail order.

333. Use luminous paint of the kind used on watches and alarm clocks to highlight figures on natural ornaments such as starfish, coral, colorful rocks, pine cones, etc. Place these in a sheltered display case to illustrate their luminosity. Have display cases on show at gift shops.

334. Begin a mail order business which promotes the hobby of collecting currency notes. Put together a catalog which lists a wide selection of currency notes and collecting accessories. Advertise in coin collecting magazines.

335. Become a clown for children's and office parties. If you have a good sense of humor and can make people laugh then this could be easy money for you.

336. Set up a business which produces a selection of novelty packets of seeds for garden weeds. These seeds might have the same as stink bombs. Sell through gift or joke shops.

337.   Design and make old fashioned country curtains. Display your curtains on a roadside stall near a busy shopping center in a similar fashion to the way double-glazing or shower firms sometimes display their products.

338.   Produce a series of videos which have titles such as: 'How to give up smoking', 'How to relax', 'How to lose weight' and 'How to sleep soundly'. Sell these by direct mail to business people. Or try to get a leading chain store to distribute them on a national basis.

339.   Reproduce old black and white or sepia photographs of a town as postcards, posters and framed prints. Have them stocked in a wide variety of shops.

340.   Design and produce your own badges. These might have designs which feature sports, witty statements, pop stars or flowers, etc. Mount on specially printed display cards and sell cards to shops.

341.   Produce a correspondence course about how to design salable knitting patterns. The main market for this would be people who want to design knitting patterns for profit rather than for enjoyment.

342.   Start a service which provides businesses with a security conscious paper collecting, shredding and disposal service. Have impressive leaflets printed to promote your service and send them to businesses.

343.   Design and manufacture kits for making string puppets. produce a selection of kits which are complementary to each other and can be used in the same puppet show.

344.   Write and publish a booklet about how to cut the cost of a wedding. Alternatively write and produce a manual about how to have a big wedding on a shoestring. Have it stocked in bookshops or sell from ads in wedding magazines.

345.   Organize bridge holidays and weekend breaks.

346.   Devise and produce a board game which simulates the experience of starting a mail order business. The usual problem of bringing out a board game is the difficulty of getting it stocked in shops. However, a game about mail order can be sold by mail order to business opportunity seekers.

347.   Bring out your own mail order catalog which is devoted to enameling craft equipment and supplies. You can commission manufacturers to make many of the supplies.

348.   Make wooden naughts and crosses games. Drill nine holes in a small square block and paint on a grid. Next make ten pegs and pint on each peg an 'O' or an 'X'. Place the grid and pegs into a clear bag and staple on a product card.

349.   Be a crossword puzzle designer who specializes in a particular subject, such as football, photography or stamp collecting. Sell football crosswords, for example, to publishers of football magazines and programs.

350.   Organize the building of reproduction stone monuments. The reasons why anyone might want a reproduction monument might include: personal gratification, an interest in the occult, to create a tourist site, to attract customers to a business, etc.

351.   Use ribbon to make souvenir pictures, for example: yellow ribbon can be used as the beach, blue as the sea, brown and green for palm trees, etc. Or design and produce kits for hobbyists. Sell by mail order or through craft shops.

352.   Begin a market stall which sells boiled sweets and hand-made chocolates. Buy your stock from small producers of confectionery.

353.   Start a mail order business which sells X-rated books. Canvass publishers at home and abroad to see if they can supply you with any books which fall into this category.

354.   Design Christmas sleigh bells for cars. These bells are attached to the exterior of a car. The motion of the car causes the bells to ring, just like sleigh bells. During the Christmas period these bells should add a pleasant seasonal flavor to cars.

355.   Employ homeworkers to make knitwear products. Go the round of retailers to find stockists.

356.   Design and make soft toys which are suitable for shelf ornaments. For example: Alice in Wonderland characters mounted on stands which have a label giving the name of each character. The high quality of workmanship should allow you to charge prices to give you a good profit.

357.   Design and have produced novelty sex maniacs score cards and find trade buyers or sell by mail order.

358.   Set up a service which reproduces family business and college crests on plaques. These might be carved, painted or

printed on each plaque. Also offer a design service. Advertise in up-market publications.

359.   Sell a wide range of postcards and souvenirs from a roadside stall.

360.   Design, make and distribute souvenir pottery doorstops. These might be imprinted with the name of a resort or a view of tourist scenery.

361.   Learn the art of tap dancing and put together your own song and dance act. Find an agent and perform at clubs, pubs and private functions.

362.   Organize the production of business greeting cards. Design the cards for a particular selection of businesses, for example, mini-cab services. The cards should have pictures relevant to the chosen business. The company can then send a card to account holders. Sell by direct mail.

363.   Rent out photocopying machines on a temporary basis. These machine might be rented by the day, week or month.

364.   Publish a newsletter about successful management. Aim the editorial at managers in large corporations. Each newsletter should discuss the issues relevant to the manager who wants to succeed.

365.   Produce an audio CD course about how to use the telephone for business. Cover subjects such as telephone selling, dealing with inquiries and complaints, interviewing, etc. Sell by direct mail and classified ads.

366.   Design and manufacture kits for making moccasins. These kits could be the basis of a mail order business. Advertise in publications read by young adults and craft magazines.

367.   Start a scarf club. Each month or quarter club members automatically receive one of the latest fashionable scarves selected by the club. Your club might have a single annual membership charge. Membership would make an ideal gift.

368.   Put together a postal service which sells personalized: golf-balls, cricket balls, snooker balls, tennis balls, etc. The exact method of placing names or initials on the balls can be worked out by you. If you can solve this problem, a lucrative market is waiting to be exploited.

369.   Start a mail order company which sells a wide range of lace. Produce a catalog which features an illustration of each design. Advertise in women's and crafts magazines.

370.   Begin a business which produces framed reprints of interesting old patents. Sell by post to professional people or have them stocked at gift shops.

371.   Start an interior decoration business which specializes in period decor. For example decor with a theme related to the Victorian or Georgian age, the 1910s, 1920s or Art Nouveau. Produce a glossy brochure about your service and use ads in up-market publications to attract inquiries.

372.   Open a school of massage. Teach, or organize the teaching of, massage to those interested in becoming professionals.

373.   Paint on wood stylistic house numbers and names. These painted numbers and names will be an attractive alternative to the traditional names burned into sliced logs. Get your work stocked at shops which sell garden products or household goods.

374.   Produce a library of audio CDs which give advice about health and psychological problems experienced by men and women. Draw up lists which are unique to men and to women. Sell by mail order.

375.   Make up pretty bags filled with aromatic herbs which are designed for hanging around the house or in cars. Add an elastic string to each bag so that one pull will release some of the aroma into the air.

376.   Consider taking up the career of chiropody. Send for a prospectus from a school of chiropody. Take a course and, after graduation, open your own practice.

377.   Produce a series of audio CDs about Confucianism. Have them stocked at health food shops and bookstores. Or sell by mail order from ads in off-beat publications.

378.   Start a theatrical enterprise which produces Christmas pantomimes. Do everything yourself, including writing the script, recruiting actors, finding a venue, organizing rehearsals, publicity and selling tickets.

379.   Bring out a correspondence course which teaches people how to be a consultant. This course should deal with every aspect of setting up a successful consultancy.

380.   Start a comprehensive garden maintenance service. discuss with clients what work needs to be done to their gardens on a regular basis. People who use your service can have a beautiful garden and not do a minute of work in it themselves.

381.   Start a newsletter for role-playing game enthusiasts. In each issue give subscribers: tips about how to win games, review new games, act as a forum for discussion about games. Sell space to display and classified advertisers.

382.   Produce a series of audio CDs about the crimes of the century. The crimes covered might include: mass murders, bank robberies, arson and fraud. Sell these CDs by direct mail, mail order or get them stocked at bookshops and newsagents.

383.   Do your own research to discover ghost stories from your region. Record the best stories on audio tape. Have the CDs duplicated and labeled and distribute to shops throughout the region covered.

384.   Bring out an audio CD course about advanced driving. Sell by mail order or get it stocked in bookshops. Or produce videos about improving driving skills and hire or sell by post. Each video might feature filmed examples of good or bad driving.

385.   Start a rent-a-horse or pony business. Horse riders, instead of keeping their own horse or pony, rent one from you.

386.   Set up a home-based computer service which maintains the mailing lists of local businesses. Also supply local businesses with mailing lists bought or rented from other firms in this country and abroad.

387.   Begin a crafts business which makes either souvenir or normal tea cosies. Find suitable retail outlets to stock your cosies. You might, for example, make souvenir tea cosies for tearooms and cafes to sell to their customers.

388.   Set up and run a school of window dressing. Organize one-day or two-day seminars for established shopkeepers who want to learn more about this aspect of their business. Also provide courses fro those who would like to take up a career as a window dresser.

389.   Compile and publish a year-book or 'Yellow Pages' type directory for those who want to start a business. In the directory list, for example: sources of finance, small business advisers, franchise companies, etc. Also sell advertising space to business opportunities promoters.

390.   Publish a monthly audio CD fro one trade, such as newsagents, grocers, hair salons, booksellers, etc. Each CD should give: Trade news, management tips, suggestions for improving sales, etc. Organize a direct mail campaign to recruit subscribers.

391.   Publish a newsletter for those who want to make money dealing in antiques. In the newsletter highlight trends in the antiques business, give tips and hints about finding bargains, tell subscribers how to sell for the highest prices, etc.

392.   Put together a regular publication which lists photographic equipment for sale. Your income comes from selling advertising space.

393.   Import specialist magazines from overseas English-speaking countries. For example: magazines relating to unusual

hobbies or sport. Your task is to build up lists of subscribers in this country. Begin by writing to overseas publishers to ask if they will supply magazines in bulk at good discount.

394.   Set up a business which teaches languages by post. The courses might consist of both audio CDs for learning to speak and written material for learning to write the language.

395.   Create a home-based debt collections service. Get a job with a debt collection agency and learn all you can before you strike out on your own. At first specialize in one type of trade and, if successful, expand into collecting debts for other trades.

396.   Open a school of rock music. Provide classes about different aspects of rock, such as singing, playing electric guitars, writing music and songs, designing stage presentations, etc. Add credibility to the school by paying established rock musicians to give many of the lessons.

397.   Bring out a newsletter which gives amateur magicians ideas for new tricks. Also sell advertising space to firms which have products to sell to amateur magicians.

398.   Start a children's badge of the month club. Attract new members by advertising in children's comics and offering a selection of free badges.

399.   Become a photographers agent. Sell the work of amateur photographers for a commission. As an agent, your knowledge of the best place to sell photographs at home and abroad could lead to some amateurs becoming published photographers.

400.   Make charming soft toy ladybirds and other insects/animals which can be attached to curtains for decoration.

401.   Have a stall which sells fashionable clothes. Your stall might be a full-time business, working at street markets or it may be part-time and appear at craft and antique fairs.

402.   Write and publish a newsletter which is devoted to profitable hobbies. The newsletter will be aimed at those who are looking for both an interesting new hobby and a way of making extra money. Asses the profit potential of a wide range of hobbies.

403.   Draw amusing cartoons of personal names at any location where there are crowds, for example: fairs, trade shows, shopping areas and tourist sites.

404.   Set up a business which promotes the making of lampshades. Lampshade making can be sold as either an interesting hobby or a business opportunity. Produce a mail order catalog of lampshade making equipment and supplies. Advertise your catalog in crafts magazines.

405.   Write and publish a manual about how to start your own book or newsletter publishing business. Sell by direct mail or from classified ads to business opportunity seekers and those interested in publishing.

406.   Begin a mail order business which sells equipment and supplies for making paper at home. Use ads in craft magazines to promote this profitable hobby.

407.   Make a selection of soft toy insects. For example: caterpillars, ladybirds, bumblebees and wasps. Package the soft toys and claim that everyone should have a pet insect.

408.   Produce a series of audio CDs which give instruction about how to mimic different accents. For example: 'Teach yourself to speak like a Texan'. Other accents might include: Yorkshire, cockney, French, English, Scottish, New York, etc.

409.   Begin a business which organizes woodcraft holidays and weekend breaks for those who want to improve and develop woodworking skills. Advertise in woodworking and crafts magazines.

410.   Design and make fashion clothes which are tailor-made to an individual's tastes. Advertise your service in trendy publications and place posters in night-clubs.

411.   Provide a sales service for oil-painters. Sell the work of artists by finding outlets and take a commission on all sales. Outlets might include: antiques shops, gift shops, private art exhibitions, overseas shops, etc.

412.   Begin an enterprise which manufactures old-fashioned, reliable flypaper. The novelty value of this old method of flying insect control suggests that it is time it enjoyed a revival.

413.   Compile and publish a bulletin which informs subscribers of photography competitions they are eligible to enter in this country and around the world. Advertise in photograph magazines.

414.   Begin a business which produces a series of teach yourself karate videos. Or bring out videos for other martial arts subjects. Sell or hire out these videos by post.

415.   Begin a business which produces a syndicated mail order catalog. Most catalogs consist of the goods of one firm. A syndicated catalog could have details of products from hundreds of suppliers.

416.   Begin a service which provides and releases doves for wedding celebrations and other special occasions.

417.   Bring out a library of audio CDs about hobby subjects such as model making, angling, stamp collecting, treasure hunting, etc. These CDs might be about specialized areas of each hobby. Sell the CDs from ads in hobby magazines or get them stocked at hobby shops.

418.   Become an importer and distributor of car accessories. Conduct thorough research in countries throughout the world to find car accessories not readily available here.

419.   Bring out a selection of men's rings which feature the name or emblem of popular football teams.

420.   Make an income by selling lucky charms at car boot sales or door-to-door. Sell, for example: Rabbits feet, horseshoes and four-leaf clovers. Start by tracking down trade sources of lucky charms.

421.   Embroider attractive designs on ladies gloves and scarves. Call on up-market retailers to persuade them to stock your products.

422.   Set up a horse-drawn minibus service in a tourist town or resort. Provide a short trip around places of interest.

423.   Start a business which records interviews with celebrities. Market these on audio CDs just as if you were selling books or records. Sell these by mail order from your own catalog and have them stocked in book and record shops.

424.   Put together a correspondence course about palmistry. Sell from ads in astrology magazines. One attraction of the course is that the palmist skills learned could be used to make money.

425.   Find a town which has a particularly high birth rate. Bottle the water drunk in that town. Sell this bottled water. The unstated implication is that the water will increase fertility.

426.   Become a portrait artist and work in a thoroughfare of a shopping or tourist area.

427.   Set up a mail order business which promotes the hobby of collecting seashells. Bring out a catalog which has a large collection of seashells, collectors accessories and books about seashells.

428.   If you have a spare room, take in a lodger or start a small-scale bed and breakfast business. If you choose the latter, either place a sign outside your house which reads 'Bed and Breakfast' or advertise in the windows of newsagents and in the classified ad columns of newspapers.

429.   Set up a health food catering service. Do the catering at a wide range of occasions such as private parties, business

functions, weddings, etc. Advertise in health food shop noticeboards and send copies of your menu to businesses.

430.   Produce a series of Whodunit audio CDs. Get your CDs stocked at bookshops and build up a reputation for producing the best whodunit CDs. Alternatively, produce a series of X-rated whodunit CDs. They can be sold by mail order.

431.   Be a diet consultant. Earn money from guiding people through published diets like the F-plan. Also you might buy the recommended food at trade prices and sell it to your clients. Advertise your service locally and visit the homes of clients to give private consultations.

432.   Start a fishing companion finding service. Take details of when an angler is available, their interests and level of skill. Offer members of your service various suitable partners. Place ads in angling publications to attract custom.

433.   Start a mail order firm which sells plans, books and supplies to origami hobbyists. Advertise your catalog in crafts magazines.

434.   Set up a postal business which offers people the chance to do all sorts of tests. Examples of tests might include: IQ, creativity, suitability to be a shop owner or entrepreneur, personality, etc. Pay experts to devise and write the tests for you.

435.   Start a publishing business which produces a guide to unusual products, services or shops. Sell by mail order or through bookshops. Also sell advertising space to some of the firms listed in your guide.

436.   Sell single roses from a roadside stall. Put up a big sign which both tempts people to buy a single rose and state the price.

437.   Bring out your own range of shawls. Increase the value of your shawls by giving each design a catchy name. Sell the shawls by mail order or get them stocked at retailers.

438.   Start a romantic time-capsule burying service. A man or woman can immortalize the one they love by having a time-capsule buried to tell future generations about their loved one.

439.   Make a selection of home-made chocolates. Rent a corner of an established shop on a Saturday to sell them.

440.   Make decorations for wine bottles. Each decoration is slipped over the neck of a bottle. These decorations are either wood carved or metal engraved with the name of a restaurant or family. Or, make floral decorations, the scent of the flowers complimenting the bouquet of the wine.

441.   Devise and invent puzzles and word games. Sell these through specialist magazines and newspapers and to book publishers.

442.   Buy and rent out steam wallpaper removing machines. Start with one fairly cheap model bought from your local DIY superstore and build up a collection.

443.   Design and make a selection of lucky charm key-rings. For example, make a key-ring fob which is a wooden or metal number seven or four-leaf clover. Mount them on a rack and have them stocked at suitable retailers.

444.   Put together a one-man theatrical show which is pleasant to watch. For example, recite highlights from Shakespeare or the work of a well-known poet. Perform your show at pubs, offices during the lunch hour, parties and private households.

445.   Use clothes pegs to make souvenir ornaments. These might take the form of animals, castles or boats, windmills and many others. Also design and produce kits so that craft-workers can make their own ornaments from clothes pegs. Sell by mail order.

446.   Design and produce mugs or posters which predict a persons future. These might be called fortune mugs (or posters). For example a mug or poster might be printed with either a reference guide to what patterns of tea leaves mean or an astrological prediction for each star sign.

447.   Hire premises at a busy tourist site and take portrait photographs of tourists. Add a novelty to the photographs by, for example, dressing the tourists up in national costume. Or dress clients in Victoriana or Wild-West garb and add a sepia, aged appearance.

448.   Be a traveling manicurist. Build up a regular round of clients at offices and private residences. Send a leaflet about your service to businesses and private residences and advertise in the local media.

449.   Begin a business which makes money from souvenir cosmetics. Bring out lipstick, for example, or hand cream which has a local theme or name. Buy from established cosmetics manufacturers and package under your own label.

450.   Set up a holiday companion introduction service. Your service matches and introduces single people who do not have anyone to go on holiday with. Place classified ads in numerous publications to attract clients. Or produce a publication which lists people who are looking for holiday companions.

451.   Compile a guide to educational and leisure holiday courses. Have this published in book form and sell by mail order and through bookshops. This has the potential for a successful annual publication.

452.   Publish a newsletter for expectant mothers. Provide subscribers with information and reassurance. Send each subscriber an issue which ties in with the stage of her pregnancy.

453.   Put together a mail order catalog of children's educational audio CDs. These might cover subjects such as spelling, reading and grammar rules, geography, history, etc. Produce some of the CDs yourself and buy others from audio publishers.

454.   Set up a service which rents out model trains, boats and planes to businesses with reception areas. These models are supposed to create goodwill because most people will look at and appreciate a good model. Your clients will include restaurants and office-based businesses and particularly travel agents.

455.   Attend pop concerts, festivals, fairs and other large public events and sell funny hats and baseball caps.

456.   Sell figure improving aids and techniques by mail order. For example, you might sell exercise programs, or products which help to remove tummy bulges or excess fat on legs.

457.   Use sliced logs to make letter racks. Slice a log and cut into two semi-circles. Take a semi-circle and stand it on it's straight side so you have the silhouette of a mound. Cut slots in the rim of the semi-circle, these slots hold the letters.

458.   Bring out novelty voodoo model brains. A voodoo model brain represents the brain of the target person and is marked with different areas such as stress, love, anxiety, pain, etc. Pins are placed in selected areas to stimulate the feelings associated with that area.

459.   If you can play a musical instrument, earn money by providing background music at: Restaurants, pubs, wine bars, tea-rooms, hotel breakfasts, amusement arcades, or ice skating rinks. Also play during the interval at theaters and/or cinemas.

460.   Start a craft business which makes enameled products such as key-ring fobs, earrings, brooches, pendants, jewelery boxes, boxes for knickknacks, etc. Sell your craft-work from a stall at markets or fairs. Or if your work is of a very high standard sell it through gift shops.

461.   Begin a business which makes cushions of unusual shapes. For example: star shaped, heart shaped, horseshoe shaped, or round with a hole in the middle.

462.   Start a central membership agency for joining fan clubs. Persuade established fan clubs to become part of your scheme. Recruit people by advertising in numerous pop and rock publications. You take a commission on all membership fees.

463.   Put together a company which publishes the bible on video. Each DVD might be devoted to a different book of the

bible. The bible might be presented by readers juxtaposed with illustrations.

464.   Publish a weekly or monthly large type newspaper for people with poor eyesight which summarizes the news of the previous week or month.

465.   Devise and organize the manufacture of cosmetics for bald heads. The vacant space on a man's bald head is not something which should be covered up but is a canvas for an artist. For example a bald head might feature wavy lines, a rainbow, sunburst, or a color to match the eyes.

466.   Make glass display cases designed to a clients requirements. The display cases might be used for models, stuffed animals or antiques. Advertise in modeling magazines and build up a list of regular clients.

467.   Design and produce lapel stickers for wearing at parties. Each sticker is printed with a statement which is designed to make it easier for guests to talk to each other, for example, 'smile if you like me'. 'Can I sip your drink?', 'You have great legs' and 'I know a secret'.

468.   Start a school of crossword puzzles. Provide tuition for people who want to either, improve their crossword skills or earn money from devising crosswords. Give tuition during the evenings and weekends. Also bring out correspondence courses on how to do and how to devise crossword puzzles.

469.   Manufacture kits for making lamp stands decorated with shells or mosaics. Bring out a selection of kits from the very

simple to the complex. Produce a catalog and use ads in crafts magazines to sell the kits by mail order.

470.   Earn from teaching people how to find a lover or life partner. You could hold classes in a hired hall, produce an audio CD course, give lessons in your home or write a manual.

471.   Publish a monthly newsletter which gives inspiration to those trying to lose weight. Successful dieting often depends on what's going on in a person's mind. A newsletter such as this can help to prepare a person, with various stories of success from those who have succeeded in losing weight and a selection of techniques to make the process easier.

472.   Have a market stall which sells inexpensive toys. Demonstrate toys to attract attention.

473.   Begin a business which hires out second-hand pin-ball machines and computer arcade games to householders. These machines might also be hired out by the night to private parties.

474.   Carve or burn into wood 'I love you' or 'Happy Birthday' messages. Sell through shops as an alternative to greetings cards. Or sell them from a stall at crafts fairs and markets.

475.   Produce a library of audio CDs about the Wild West. Sell by direct mail or have them stocked in bookshops and record shops.

476.   Produce a series of audio CDs about how to stop or reduce vices and bad habits. The CDs might have titles like : 'How to Stop Snoring', 'How to Cut Down on Drinking', 'How to Pack Up

Gambling', 'How to Stop Smoking', etc. Sell the CDs by mail order and through a wide range of shops.

477.   Begin a word and phrase origin finding service. This service would be invaluable to academics, lecturers, authors and all others curious about the origin of words and phrases.

478.   Have an undergarments market stall and sell: men's underwear, socks, tights, stockings, fancy lingerie, long johns, etc.

479.   Devise and produce biblical role playing games. For example, people might take the roles of characters in parables. Arrange for the games to be manufactured. Sell by post or get them stocked at shops, particularly shops specializing in religion.

480.   Use various fabrics to make money belts of your own design. Attach each money belt to a printed card and sell these fully stocked to shoe repair shops and newsagents.

481.   Design a range of blank achievement certificates for use by sports clubs and schools. Have them printed and sell by direct mail.

482.   Put together a range of noticeboards for displaying things like: Staff notices, fire instructions, health and safety rules, productivity figures, etc. Call on businesses to sell the noticeboards and include a free installation service in your offer.

483.   Design and make fashionable clothes for children. You might sell them direct or through agents at party plan.

484.   Start a fortune telling gift service for new born babies. When a baby is born a fortune-teller provides a written statement

about their future. Such a statement would make an ideal birth gift. Advertise in the classified columnist of a variety of publications.

485.	Start a service which does postal auditions of voices and music. A person records his or her voice on a CD and sends it to you. Or a group records their music. You make an assessment of the performance for a fee. Advertise your service in music publications.

486.	Set up a firm which provides tours of the underside of a big city. Your tour might visit: streets where prostitutes and drug dealers wait for clients, skid row, a main rubbish tip, crime-ridden neighborhoods, etc. Give your tour a name like 'Shocking side of the city'.

487.	Start a singles contact magazine or newsletter, each issue might include both small ads from people looking for partners and editorials of interest to single people. Use press and magazine advertising to build up a list of subscribers.

488.	Put together a hamper of children's jokes and novelties. In each hamper include many of the products popular with children such as trick matches, itching powder, plastic spiders, etc. Get small hampers stocked at toy shops and newsagents. Sell larger hampers by mail order.

489.	Organize tours of well-known sights or areas of outstanding natural beauty. Buy or rent an open topped bus for the tours. Also use this bus for weddings, work excursions and school trips.

490.   Write, produce and sell a correspondence course about inventing for profit. The course would help a person to develop creative abilities and identifies areas where small inventors get the most patents. A key selling point of your course is that inventing is both fun and lucrative.

491.   Start a special effects rental service. Hire out machines which make bubbles, wind, fog, falling snow or flashing lights. Your custom will come from private parties, night-clubs, theaters, pop groups and film companies. Also, if required, provide a person to operate the machines.

492.   Give private tuition about how to make money. The tuition might be about making money from business and investments. You might, for example, use some of the ideas listed in this selection as worthwhile money-makers. Prepare lesson plans on the subjects you wish to cover and teach a set course.

493.   Arrange for a set of pictures to be printed to look like old cigarette cards. Turn out hundreds of framed sets and sell to wholesalers and gift shops.

494.   Sell smoke detectors door-to-door. Expand by using sales personnel to sell for you.

495.   Start a mail order business which sells books about how to win at gambling. The games covered might include: roulette, baccarat, poker and horse-racing. Buy the publications direct from publishers at home and abroad. Or publish the books yourself.

496.   Design and manufacture wooden kits for constructing model boats. Sell from ads in hobby magazines or have them stocked in modeling and crafts shops.

497.   Begin a business which makes up bottle gardens. To make your gardens distinctive, find bottles of an interesting and unusual design. Get them stocked at shops which do not usually stock such products. For example: health food shops and grocers.

498.   Start a bookplates of the month club for both established collectors and for people who would like to take up a new collecting hobby. The bread and butter work of this club would involve sending newly issued bookplates to club members.

499.   Set up a mail order business which sells second-hand books. Use your own books for the initial stock. Find further stock by advertising for both trade source and complete collections from private individuals. Produce lists and place ads in various magazines.

500.   Set up a direct mail business which sells business books. This type of business offers the greatest potential for profit if you publish the books you sell. Do this by 1) Writing a book of your own; 2) Advertising for authors' manuscripts; and 3) Contacting literary agents.

501.   Help people to get jobs by starting a C.V. design service. Conduct your own research into what information in a C.V. impresses employers. Basically, a good C.V. is professionally printed and presents the most important facts about a persons career history in a simple, clear way.

502.   Start a postal business which rents out war gaming model soldiers and other accessories. War gaming enthusiasts can use this service to play war games of any size from any period of history.

503.   Produce a correspondence course about how to write biography. Biography publishing is one of the largest sectors of the book industry.

504.   Create a mail order business which sells drinking accessories and memorabilia, for example, yard-long drinking glasses, personalized tankards, traditional pub games, collectable beer mats, books about drinking and breweries.

505.   Start an interior decoration business which specializes in Tudor. Your service might include fitting ornamental oak beams and providing iron and brass wall ornaments. Put together a sales presentation and advertise in up-market magazines.

506.   Design and produce a stock market investors log book. The purpose of this log book is to record and chart: the prices of individual shares, purchases, sales, dealing costs, profits and losses. Sell by mail order and direct mail to investors.

507.   Start a mail order business which specializes in selling information and plans about cave systems in this country and abroad. Produce a catalog about what you have for sale and advertise in potholing and outdoor adventure publications.

508.   Set up a company director exchange service. Your service arranges for one or two directors in different companies to swap places at board meetings. Use telephone or direct mail to sell your service to businesses.

509.   If you are physically attractive, become a freelance escort. Place adverts in local papers which state you will accompany an unattached person to social or business functions.

510.	Produce an audio CD or booklet which is about past major crimes in your area. Do research at local libraries and newspaper archives. Have your products stocked at local shops. You might give your CD or booklet a title like 'Your Town's Top 30 Crimes'.

511.	Use unusual materials to make names of football teams for hanging on walls. For example they might be made from lines of studs on leather. Sell from ads in football magazines and programs.

512.	Call door-to-door and offer to buy unwanted furniture. Or use local media to advertise your interest in buying second-hand furniture. Sell what you buy from free ads in local papers, or start your own second-hand furniture shop.

513.	One of the characteristics of sexual attraction is that people are often fascinated by one part of the body such as legs, build or faces. Start a mail order business which sells slides, photographs and posters about legs, for example, or faces.

514.	Make a selection of soft toy or fabric luggage tags. For example, a normal luggage tag is accompanied by two small dice made from soft toy materials. Alternatively make a range of soft toy luggage tags which are designed to act as travel mascots.

515.	Set up a mail order business which sells motorcycle memorabilia. Put together a catalog which includes: videos, films, posters, photographs, books, instruction booklets, old magazines and newspapers, etc. Advertise your catalog in motorcycle magazines.

516.	Buy original computer games programs from home computer enthusiasts. Find these programs by advertising in computing magazines. Produce a compilation of the programs on a master floppy disk. Have copies of this disk made and sell from ads in home computing magazines.

517. Start a general sports tuition agency. Either provide clients with a tutor to give individual tuition or organize courses for different sports and sell places on each course. Produce a leaflet about your service and get copies displayed at sports shops.

518. Make soft toy lucky charms. One idea is a giant number seven. Other ideas include: four leaf clovers, horseshoes, rabbits feet and destiny dice.

519. Publish an audio CD of saucy seaside jokes. Sell through shops at seaside resorts. The hope is that holiday-makers might send a saucy CD home instead of a saucy postcard. With each CD include a small card for writing a message.

520. Begin a mail order business which sells boxing memorabilia. Start this business by finding a trade source of boxing films and videos. Or obtain the rights to reproduce boxing films and videos.

521. Design a sport log book so that sport enthusiasts can keep a record of their performance. Get copies printed and sell to shops or sell from ads in sports magazines.

522. Set up a quiz games postal club. Club members compete against each other to win quizzes through the mail. The quizzes could be published in a regular newsletter which would also give the answers to the previous newsletters quiz(zes).

523. Begin a venture which arranges for business and sales meetings to take place at exotic and unusual venues. For example, a businessman can negotiate a contract with a client at a castle, or on a yacht or in a sightseeing plane.

524. Make life-size string puppets. Each puppet is controlled by someone standing on a roof, balcony or scaffold. Use for promotion or entertainment.

525. Start a top 20 chart for witty and arty T-shirts. Distribute copies of the chart and the top 20 T-shirts to a wide range of retailers.

526. Write and publish a manual about how to make money from property. In the manual include chapters on: Buying and selling land, buying properties for conversions and renovations, investing in property, etc. Use direct mail and press advertising to sell by mail order to business opportunity seekers.

527. Bring out a DVD which consists of a long recording of an open fire. By playing the video anyone can have the charm of an open fire in their home without the mess and the hassle.

528. Design and make fashionable jump suits. Make the rounds of boutiques to find suitable stockists.

529. Write to overseas publishers of English language newsletters and offer to act as the distributor for their newsletter in this country. In your letter to the publishers outline the benefits they will gain if they let you distribute their newsletter.

530.   Make hand-painted badges. These might feature: a tiny traditional painting, an abstract painting, witty statements, popular symbols and funny faces.

531.   Design and have printed novelty joke licenses. Each license has a space for a name to be added. The license may state that the named person is: a genius, certified insane, international sex maniac, etc. Distribute to shops which sell souvenirs, jokes and gifts.

532.   Do your own research to discover the secrets of conjuring. Write a manuscript about your findings and publish it yourself. The novel and sensational nature of this book will ensure that it sells well from ads in newspapers and magazines.

533.   Put together an audio CD course about teach yourself the Welsh language. Sell the course by mail order and get it stocked at bookshops and souvenir shops throughout Wales.

534.   Learn and then teach origami. Also, if you have a flair for making artifacts in an interesting way, earn money from doing origami as entertainment.

535.   Put together your own catalog of jewelery making supplies. Locate the sources of products by doing the routine work of the mail order trader: write to potential suppliers. Throughout the country there are thousands of craft-workers who would welcome a new catalog.

536.   Cut chess pieces into slices and use them to make earrings, necklaces and key-ring fobs. Sell at craft work markets and fairs.

537.   Start a business which organizes snooker holidays and weekend breaks. During each holiday or break provide guests with tuition from a professional snooker player.

538.   Bring out an educational newsletter about 'How to Improve Your Written English'. Each monthly newsletter might be like a lesson. There are only a limited number of lessons, so you can send the same series to different subscribers for many years.

539.   Produce a selection of postcards which feature traditional oil paintings of tourist sites. The paintings featured might be contemporary or historical.

540.   Deal in antique and reproduction dolls, and dolls houses. Build up relationships with collectors so that you know where to sell any new items that you acquire. Also produce a mail order catalog of reproduction dolls.

541.   Start a service which commissions artists to do drawings of business premises or private residences. Also arrange for the drawings to be reproduced on: stationery, postcards, calendars, business cards, etc. Advertise in business publications and also do work for established printers.

542.   Be a home-visiting pre-school teacher. Your task is to prepare children for a successful start at school.

543.   Make good, old-fashioned wooden tool carriers and have them stocked at hardware shops and tool shops. Or produce kits for making tool carriers and sell by mail order from ads in DIY magazines.

544.   Put together a spoon bending act that is inspired by Uri Geller. Get yourself an agent and earn money from performing at a wide range of venues such as clubs, pubs, theaters, private parties, etc.

545.   Rent computers to private business users. The computers you rent might be new and/or second hand. Also rent out peripherals such as printers, stands and sheet feeders. Use local media to inform potential customers about your service.

546.   Design a log book for cooks. In this log book a cook records what recipes were tested and comments on the result. Pay to have the log book printed and sell from ads in women's magazines.

547.   Manufacture kits for making mosaics. Each kit will have a pre-designed mosaic and people will have to complete it like a jigsaw puzzle. Use ads in craft magazines to sell kits by mail order.

548.   Publish a book which lists recipes for making nutritious dog food and biscuits. Sell to discerning dog owners through dog magazines, pet shops and bookstores.

549.   Sell novelty trays of British soil to expatriates. This can be applied to any other nationals. Stick a tiny national flag in the soil of each tray.

550.   Produce colored acetate paper printed with painting by number designs for shops. The designs could include elaborate 'sale' signs and pictures with a Christmas theme. A shopkeeper sticks the acetate sheets to one side of a window and paints the design or picture on the other.

551.　Set up a market stall at a tourist town which sells all kinds of belts from the highly fashionable to the personalized.

552.　Open a market stall which sells hats and other headgear. Your stock will include: ladies hats, scarves, men's caps and Balaclava helmets.

553.　Make a selection of balaclava helmets in the colors of popular football teams or the national flag. Sell from roadside stall on route to football ground, or through supporters clubs.

554.　Start a newsletter for diarists. Diarists nearly all work in isolation and many would welcome a newsletter to inform them about the existence and activities of their fellow diarists. The newsletter may act as a forum for discussion about diary writing and also give advice about how to improve upon the technique of diary writing.

555.　Start a mail order business which sells paper and card products to photographers. For example, sell stationery with a photographic theme, cardboard frames in bulk at a discount price, printed paper with frames for planning photograph collections, paper supplies for processing, etc.

556.　Start a business which makes garden hammocks. Devise your own hammock which has at least one superior feature over other hammocks available. Sell through hardware shops and garden centers and by mail order from ads in gardening publications.

557.　Publish a booklet which provides a lengthy list of mottoes for use by: societies, clubs, institutions, families and individuals. Have the booklet stocked at shops. Also start a postal service which devises mottoes. Use a page in the booklet to advertise your postal service.

558.　Start a business which delivers bulky pet food direct to the public. Build up a round of regular customers. Call on houses throughout your area to sell your service.

559.　Produce a series of music and sound effects audio CDs which are specially designed to aid the growth of household plants. For example, sounds might include the wind blowing and birds singing. Advertise in gardening and householders magazines.

560.　Produce an audio CD course about positive thinking. Sell by direct mail and through press advertising.

561.　Write and produce a correspondence course about how to start and build a successful craft business. Subjects covered by the course might include: How to choose and design a winning product, how to sell craft-work, how to use other craft-workers in your business, etc.

562.　Make money from bringing out your own happiness plants. A happiness plant is any plant for which it can be claimed gives off an unseen aura or odor which humans find pleasing. Sell from a market stall or by mail order.

563.　Learn about the craft of making ornaments with eggshells. Make money from what you learn by bringing together a selection of supplies for selling to egg craft hobbyists.

564.   Organize the production and distribution of souvenir potted plant holders. These plant holders should appeal to the same people who buy souvenir trays.

565.   Create a folder of sample sales letters for all occasions. The letters might sell: advice, maintenance, products, a service which gives free quotes, etc. Sell these folders by direct mail to small businesses.

566.   Bring together a selection of supplies for making string puppets and start a mail order business. There is already a thriving market in doll making supplies. Your business will hopefully divert some people from making dolls to making string puppets.

567.   Write a non-fiction book which may, for example, be about a hobby. Enlist a book printer to produce copies of the book. Sell these to the market that would be interested in the contents. You might, for example, place ads in hobby magazines.

568.   Produce and sell a home study course on how to write self-improvement books. Writing this type of book is one of the easiest ways to become a published author. In this field there are always themes which sell well, such as how to make money, attract love and how to be a success.

569.   Take a course in basketry. As you develop your skill slowly begin to sell what you make. When your work reaches a high enough standard, go into business full-time.

570.   Package freshly or specially hardened conkers and sell through newsagents and toy shops. Each pack might contain 4-6 conkers.

571.   Buy a selection of local history books, pamphlets, posters and postcards from the publishes at trade prices. Earn from selling these door-to-door in your area.

572.   Open a school of creativity. Teach business people about the various techniques of creative thinking such as brainstorming, lateral thinking, quick think, value analysis, etc. Hold classes or give personal tuition during work hours or lunch breaks.

573.   Begin a business which produces horror novelty wall-hangings. For example, a framed picture which has the picture itself covered by a sliding or hinged door. The door can be opened to reveal a scary scene. Another example would be a wall mirror with the faint face of a ghost peering out.

574.   Act as a sales agent for fan clubs. Sell memberships for a commission at concerts, festivals, and to people in your area. Write to fan clubs to offer this service.

575.   Set up a postal enterprise which sells signed photographs of celebrities. Or, if a particular celebrity is in demand, offer to donate money to charity if X number of signed photographs are sent to you.

576.   Set up a mail order business which specializes in selling videos, films, photographs, posters and slides about the pop music of the 50s and60s. Use your ingenuity to find products, for example canvass picture libraries and record and film companies.

577.   Frame photographs of well known boxers. Get these stocked at sports shops or sell by mail order from ads in boxing and sports papers and magazines.

578.	Hand-paint pictures or witty statements on small squares of wood. For example, the pictures might feature animals and the statements might be about cooking like 'Oliver Twist's Favorite Kitchen'. Add a magnet to the back of each square so that they can be stuck to fridges and other metallic surfaces.

579.	Start a mail order firm which sells equipment and supplies to weavers and spinners. An important market will be those taking up weaving and spinning for the first time. Place ads in crafts magazines which are directed at this group.

580.	Select a range of lingerie and sell it by party plan. Once you develop a winning formula, build up your business by recruiting and training agents to sell your range of products.

581.	Bring out a selection of computer programs which can be sold as a business opportunity. For example, one program might be for starting a computerized dating agency, another for writing a newsletter or classified ad sheet, a third for starting a computerized marketplace.

582.	Make either, commemorative wall-hanging tapestries or reproduce parts of the Bayeux tapestry. Use press advertising to sell these as highly collectible artifacts.

583.	Have amusing messages printed in speech bubbles on the sides of potted plant holders. For example: 'Hello, my name is...', 'Shake my water, don't stir it', 'I feel like a chat', etc. Have these stocked at outlets which sell garden products.

584.	Produce a selection of political and moral T-shirts. These will be designs to publicly express a persons opinion. Sell at demonstrations and through ads in the political press. Also bring out a mail order catalog.

585. Sell Jazz memorabilia by post. Start a world-wide search for products to put in your catalog. The products might include: photographs, slides, posters, old magazines, duplicate press cuttings, books, DVD and audio CDs.

586. At tourist sites take photographs of holiday makers with a man dressed as a gorilla, or other amusing costume.

587. Use cheese-cloth to make your own range of fashion clothes such as blouses, skirts and shirts.

588. Set up a mail order business which sells equipment and supplies for making herbal drinks at home. This could be an interesting and healthy hobby for anyone to take up. Produce a small catalog and advertise in a wide range of publications.

589. Write and publish a series of manuals about starting and running a variety of crafts businesses. Examples of crafts covered might include: leather work, soft toy making, pottery, woodcarving, and egg crafts. Sell through classified ads or have stocked in craft shops.

590. There seems to be an insatiable demand for quality, novel or inexpensive clocks. If you want to start an import business, this would be a suitable area to try.

591. Open a stall in an antiques market which sells collectable plates. Buy your stock of plates from manufacturers, wholesalers and collectors.

592.   Start a general problem solving service for personal affairs. This service acts like a private agony aunt. An expert is provided to deal with the problem your client is trying to solve. The expert might give advice by telephone, by post or in person.

593.   Devise a selection of scents specially designed for love letters and greeting cards. For example, the scent of roses for love letters and pine trees for Christmas cards. Set up a business which manufactures, packages and distributes the scents.

594.   Make, mount and frame models of butterflies. The wings are either hand painted or printed. The body of the butterfly might be made of casting metal. The finished model butterflies may be sold through gift or souvenir shops.

595.   Begin and build a weed removal and control round. Operate this like a window cleaning service. You might do this work yourself or employ students or retired people.

596.   Begin a business which produces correspondence courses about home computing. Base each course on a popular software application and have a general course on general computer operation. The lessons in your course might be modeled on what already exists in textbooks. Sell from ads in computer magazines.

597.   Start a novel sedan chair service in the center of a tourist town. Carry a tourist on a short tour of the city center.

598.   Commission the drawing of political cartoons which have an anti-establishment theme. Have these printed on postcards or posters and sell through shops popular with young adults.

599.   Decorate everyday objects with pressed flowers. Add an inlaid design of pressed flowers to trays, coasters, jewelery boxes, paperweights, picture frames, wall-hangings, desk sets and table tops.

600.   Start a mail order business which sells health improvement books, booklets and audio CDs. Discover what titles are available from publishers and produce your own catalog. Also publish some of your own booklets and CDs.

601.   Invent and develop a program which is designed to turn a failure into a successful person. The program might take the form of a series of booklets, loose-leaf binders of information, or a correspondence course. Sell your program from ads in newspapers and magazines.

602.   Bring together a selection of the best business audio CDs from the previous year. Start a direct mail campaign which offers these CDs to businesspeople at a reduced rate if they buy the set.

603.   Start a mail order business which sells stop smoking aids. For example: dummy cigarettes, advice booklets, herbal aids, inspirational CDs, charts and posters. You can produce many of these products yourself and buy the others from wholesalers.

604.   Set up a service which organizes theme parties and banquets. The theme of each party might be, for example: medieval, Wild West or horror. You organize everything for the evening, such as the music, entertainers, costumes, props, waiting staff, food, cutlery, etc.

605.   Do alterations and repairs for dry cleaning services, menswear shops, factories and offices. Visit these places and

inform them of your services. Offer, for example, to collect the goods once or twice a week.

606.   Make energy saving 'sausages'. Fill a sausage shaped bag with sand so that it can be placed against a draughty door or window. Sell door-to-door or have them sold in hardware shops. Also sell kits by mail order.

607.   Bottle sand from the beach where William the Conqueror landed in 1066 and sell to those who want to buy a piece of history.

608.   Rent out stuffed and mounted birds, fish and other animals. Your clients might include: restaurants, breweries, clubs, travel agents and other businesses with reception areas.

609.   Bring out kits for making relief pictures with wood. For example, a kit for making a rural scene might include wooden pieces cut in the shape of: trees, animals, clouds, buildings, etc. Sell either by mail order to craft-workers or through shops which sell craft products.

610.   Make wooden puzzles for children. For example, brightly painted wooden shapes have to be fitted into the corresponding hole in a block of wood. Or make a flat wooden animal like a dinosaur or rabbit. Cut this animal into lots of wooden shapes so that it is a challenge to assemble.

611.   Produce book markers which have attractive embroidered designs. Package them in cellophane and have them stocked at bookshops.

612.   Start a school of English and give lessons to an ethnic group who want to improve their written and spoken English. You might give tuition either in your own home or at hired premises.

613.   Write and publish a newsletter for those who want to start a successful business. The newsletter might, for example, discuss effective ways of: Selling, managing, generating ideas, locating suppliers and finding customers. Use your local library service to research these topics.

614.   Sell ideas and recipes for making unusual cakes. For example cakes shaped like: cars, UFOs, trains, ships, famous landmarks, etc. For each design produce a folded page, like a knitting pattern. Sell these printed patterns through outlets which sell cake decorations.

615.   Start a service which finds companions for those who want to go on cycling or hiking holidays. Advertise in publications for cyclists or hikers.

616.   If you live near a port or marina. Start and operate a boat and yacht valeting service. Seek expert advice from someone knowledgeable about boating or yachting and what is involved in marine valeting.

617.   Sell greenhouses door-to-door. Buy the greenhouses from manufacturers at trade prices. Produce sales literature and recruit sales people to sell the greenhouses for you.

618.   Frame and label samples of many different metals. At a glance the physical appearance of different metals can be

compared. Sell by direct mail to engineering companies, scientists, schools and metalwork hobbyists.

619.   Learn the art of I Ching. Then, earn a sideline income by persuading party hosts to pay you to give readings to guests.

620.   Do bottle art. Paint local scenery and other artistic images on the exterior of tiny bottles. Sell as souvenirs or ornaments.

621.   Become an astrologer who specializes in producing charts and readings for babies, children and teenagers. You might, for example, use astrology to provide career advise for teenagers. Do charts and readings by post and also do personal consultations with parents.

622.   Bring out a range of herbal or hop filled pillows. Make pillows for different functions, for example: pillows which are an aid for people who have difficulty sleeping, siesta pillows for the garden nap, pillows for the living room and pillows which are especially designed for daydreaming.

623.   Deal in the antiques and memorabilia of an ethnic group. Put together a catalog which features: history books, videos, antiques, prints and ephemera. Examples of suitable ethnic groups include: Polish, Italian, West Indian, Scottish, Irish, Native North American, Indian, etc, etc, etc.

624.   Set up a business which organizes record, stamp or book fairs. Find a venue, sell places to stall holders by placing ads in hobby magazines and publicize to attract customers.

625.   Set up a business which sends British comics to both expatriates and overseas collectors of British comics. You might

send comics on a weekly basis as they are published, save them up and post every quarter or advertise world-wide offering a sample of British comics.

626. Pay a taxidermist to prepare, stuff and mount fish. Produce a mail order catalog about your mounted fish. Advertise in angling publications. Also sell through gift shops and fishing tackle shops.

627. Put together an educational pack which contains samples of many types of wood. Use direct mail to sell this educational pack to woodworkers, schools and colleges.

628. Put together a range of lucky charms. Mount these on printed cards or counter-top racks and distribute to newsagents and gift shops.

629. Open a school of antique restoration. Offer potential students a choice of courses covering most aspects of restoration. Potential students will include antique collectors and dealers. Advertise in magazines about antiques.

630. Start a training school which specializes in teaching the art of sketching. Use sketch artists to do the teaching. Your job is to find students and organize the premises and management. Also put together a postal course which teaches sketching to beginners.

631. Start a theatrical play of the month club. Operate this like a book club but sell only theatrical plays. The club will not offer discounts on publications, but you can send copies of the latest plays opening at theaters.

632.   Produce a selection of posters which feature photographs of elaborate models. Mount these on display units and get model shops to show them.

633.   Sell copies of theatrical plays by post. Put together a wide range of new and second-hand publications and produce a catalog. Advertise your catalog in both the theater press and theater programs.

634.   Produce and sell novelty hate or confession bags. These are like sick bags except people talk or shout into them. They get something out of their system and consequently feel better.

635.   Write and publish a letter about moonlighting. Give subscribers ideas about moonlighting ventures. Also include articles about subjects such as how to cope with a full-time job, how to manage your income and how to turn a part-time venture into a full-time business.

636.   Start a mail order business which promotes the craft of making ornaments and models from shaping wire. Design and make up a complete kit for beginners. Include this kit in your catalog, as well as tools, design ideas and raw materials for wire craft workers.

637.   Set up a window cleaning round and employ students and other young people to do the work. Build up lots of individual rounds and employ a person for each one.

638.   Start a newspaper clipping bureau. Do work for firms who want a comprehensive collection of press clippings about news and developments in their field. Have leaflets printed about your

service and sent them to firms. As an incentive offer firms a free trial period.

639.   Add a stand to small cubes of marble and sell as ornaments.

640.   Design souvenir badges which read 'I've been to (name of town)' or 'I love ....'. Pay to have your badges professionally made. Arrange for shops in the named town to stock these badges.

641.   Earn a small regular income from renting out part of your garden to someone who wants to grow food. Thus a part of your garden will become a private allotment.

642.   Write and publish an annual directory about 'penny shares'. The purpose is to examine the performance of penny shares companies over the past year. Sell by direct mail to investors, have stocked in bookshops and advertise in investment magazines.

643.   specialize in organizing trips to vineyards and beer festivals. Issue an annual or quarterly brochure which gives full details of all the holidays you are planning. Advertise in beer and wine publications.

644.   Bring out a board game about buying and running a shop. The shop might be a newsagent or the game might involve several types of shops. Sell from ads in publications which list shops for sale.

645.   Use direct mail to sell a range of novelties, games, toys, quizzes and ornaments for the office. Produce a catalog and send to offices.

646.   Devise and produce an easy-to-use system for cataloging coin collections. Sell this through stamp and coin shops, or from ads in collectors magazines.

647.   Bring out X-rated cardboard cut-outs of female or male models. Sell by mail order from ads in adult magazines.

648.   Produce a selection of small posters of dogs and cats. Have these stocked at pet shops and gifts shops. For example, at pet shops have a sample of each poster covered by a transparent plastic. Hang these from a rack and have the salable posters in rolls in a basket underneath.

649.   Use a horse and carriage to take tourists on sightseeing tours.

650.   Start a business which organizes cricket holidays and weekend breaks. During these breaks arrange for guests to receive tuition from a professional cricketer.

651.   Create a mail order business which sells matchboxes and labels to collectors. Collectors automatically receive the latest matchboxes each month. Alternatively you might put together a catalog of old and rare matchboxes.

652.   Design and produce animation kits for amateur film makers, each kit consists of numerous paper characters with moveable joints and a selection of background scenery. An

amateur film maker can use a kit to make hobby and animation films. A kit might have, for example, a Wild West theme.

653.   Start a postal business which sells novel birth and death certificates to those who like to claim that they had previous lives. Design the certificates yourself and pay for them to be printed. Also offer a service which uses occult methods to identify previous lives.

654.   Publish a craft-workers' equivalent to the 'Yellow Pages'. In the directory include the addresses of sources for a wide range of products. List the addresses under a heading for each craft. Also sell advertising space to suppliers, crafts schools, craft-workers, etc.

655.   In a city where there are many theaters, open a small shop which is devoted to selling things related to Shakespeare.

656.   Found a trade publication for publishers of audio CDs. This publication should give the latest news about this industry. Also accept ads from businesses who want to sell products to audio CD publishers.

657.   Begin a mail order business which promotes the craft of making Jack-in-the-boxes. In your catalog include a wide selection of: springs, boxes, design plans, materials for making the character in the box, etc. Advertise in crafts magazines.

658.   Make videos for people who want to sell their business. Each video is designed to show a business in its best light. In the video, interview customers, look at its standing in the community, etc. Your video should help achieve the highest possible sale price for the businesses whose sale you promote.

659.   Produce an aerial video of your area. Duplicate this and have it stocked at video hire shops and other local shops.

660.   Start a crafts business which uses interesting foreign coins to make jewelery. Incorporate coins into pendant bracelet, brooches, necklaces and earrings. Alternatively, make jewelery which features reproduction coins from the ancient world.

661.   Bring out a range of jewelery for ears. However, this jewelery does not hang from earlobes like earrings, but gently clips to the top of the ears. This jewelery looks as if it if it is perched on top of the ears. A piece of ear-top jewelery might follow the curvature of each ear.

662.   Start a dating agency or marriage bureau specially for the separated or divorced. Use local advertising to attract clients.

663.   Set up an enterprise which organists the publishing of vanity poetry books. Poets pay you to have their work published in a professional manner. Each book might contain the work of one or more poets.

664.   Write and publish a monthly newsletter which helps those who want to give up smoking. The ability to give up smoking depends what's happening in a persons mind. A good newsletter could make the difference between success and failure.

665.   Make rosettes. Add to each rosette either a calligraphed or printed label which reads 'Cook of the Year', 'Prize Winning Mother', or 'Dad of the Year'. Have them displayed in local shops.

666.   If you are an expert on crafts, earn money from teaching it in quite corners or back rooms of shops which sell wools, crafts, artists materials or picture framing services.

667.   Start a company which organizes business anniversary celebrations. Devise celebration packages and sell to businesses who have been trading for 1, 5, 10, 20, 21, 25, 50, 60, 75, or 100 years. Locate potential clients by searching records located at Companies House to discover when firms were formed.

668.   Set up a business which organizes weight loss holidays. These holidays are not on health farms but consist of long distance walking, diet instruction, and discussion amongst participants. A person who wants to lose weight goes on a two or four week holiday which would consist of walking for most of the day, following a strict diet and evenings of discussion groups.

669.   Take imaginative photographs of landscapes, cityscapes and people. Enlarge the best of these and frame them. Display at arts and crafts fairs and sell as photographic art.

670.   Deal in collectible bookplates. Promote the hobby of collecting bookplates by offering potential collectors a free selection. Thereafter send collectors a regular list of bookplates for sale. Also bring out and sell albums for storing and displaying bookplates.

671.   Start a school for pop or rock group management. Your students will include those who aspire to become a manager or leader of a pop or rock group. The course might be taught by post or held as a class.

672.   Use logs and wood to make small ornamental garden wishing wells. Sell through garden centers and hardware shops.

673.   Start a school of hydroponic gardening. The aims of your school might include: publishing booklets, producing audio CDs, organizing holiday courses, giving personal tuition and selling supplies.

674.   Bring out a booklet which has a title like "1001 Unusual Facts About Your Town". Discover these facts by reading local history books and visiting the archives of local newspapers. You could do similar booklets about a variety of towns and specialize in those which are popular with tourists.

675.   Produce a series of audio CDs or booklets about the folklore of your region. Have them stocked at local shops.

676.   Set up a direct mail postal library. For a fee any business can borrow examples of previous direct mail campaigns. A client business might borrow the work of either competitors or potential clients.

677.   Hang low cost, imported leather belts on racks. Get various shops to take a rack of belts.

678.   Set up a service which gives independent valuations and assessments for those considering the purchase of a particular expensive antique.

679.   Bring out a series of booklets or CDs about how to get rid of, or escape the attentions of various types of people such as: unsatisfactory employers, salesmen, bores, fools, unwanted

admirers, officials, etc. Sell the booklets or CDs as a complete set by mail order or through bookshops.

680.   Begin a business which bottles sea or lake water. Sell the bottles as either souvenirs, i.e. 'pocket or desktop Atlantic Ocean' or a natural beauty treatment, i.e. 'bathe your face in natural lake water'.

681.   Open a television and video school. Organize practical courses in television and video production. Buy a second-hand closed circuit television system, rent or lease a hall and use this as the premises of the school.

682.   Use low value foreign coins to make unusual pictures. For example, might be either a coin mosaic or a selection of coins mounted next to each other to make silhouettes of landscapes. Frame the pictures and get them stocked at shops which sell gifts, coins or souvenirs.

683.   Bring out folders specially designed to hold sheet music or knitting patterns. Sell these from either, suitable shops or ads in publications read by people who collect sheet music or knitting patterns.

684.   Make leather folders for salespeople to use when making presentations. Have these stocked a stationers or produce a catalog about your range of folders and send it to businesses.

685.   Seek out as many recipes as you can for nougat. Devise, with the help of these, your own brand of delicious nougat. Have sizable quantities made and sell from a stall or get it stocked at shops.

686.   Begin a business which sells exotic plants to image conscious local businesses. Call office-to-office and offer to bring a selection of plants on a trial basis, for example 10 days, free approval without obligation.

687.   Sell home-made bubble mixture to children at markets, roadside sites, fairgrounds and fetes. Give each child a ring made from soft wire to make the bubbles with.

688.   Bring out a selection of souvenir ties. The ties might feature the name or emblem of a holiday resort. Mount the ties on racks and get them displayed in shops which sell souvenirs.

689.   Earn money from anatomical charts. Use the charts to : 1) Make stylish framed prints. 2) Make unusual designs for T-shirts. 3) Decorate household products such as wastepaper bins and lampshades. 4) Make decorative or educational posters. or 5) Make a collection of educational slides.

690.   Found a year-book for people who do creative things with their hands, such as painters, drawers, sculptors, cartoonists, illustrators, cartoonists, engravers, etc. Also list buyers of art, art schools, art fairs, etc. Have the year-book stocked at bookshops, artists supplies shops, craft shops and sell by mail.

691.   Write and publish a manual about how to bring out a correspondence course. For many people this could be a route to a business which both provides enough money to live on and doesn't require much money to set up. Sell the manual to business opportunity seekers.

692.   Make fashionable patchwork sweaters and have them stocked at shops. Alternatively, sell the sweaters from a stall at a market fair.

693.   Earn an income from being a freelance salesperson. Place ads in business or trade publications which reads 'Freelance Salesperson Available. Anything Considered. Contact.....'. Don't accept the first offer, but consider each one and accept the one you find the most suitable.

694.   Begin a mail order business which sells a selection of products of particular interest to motorbike enthusiasts. In your catalog include; badges, clothing, cult ornaments, etc. Advertise in motorbike magazines.

695.   Design and manufacture desks for putting on laps in cars. These should be lightweight and easy to store in a car. They might be used by sales people to make notes about calls, business people to prepare for meetings and passengers to work from whilst traveling.

696.   Produce a correspondence course which is designed to improve a persons standard of general knowledge. In your advertising emphasize that a better life might result from taking the course.

697.   Start a business which designs and manufactures simple basketry kits for beginners. Have them stocked at crafts shops or sell by mail order in crafts magazines.

698.   Open a computerized marketplace for cars and motorbikes. On computer list the sellers and what they have to sell. Charge the sellers a fee for this service. Place ads which

invite people who want to buy a car or bike to telephone you to see if you have what they want.

699.   Begin a mail order firm which promotes the collecting of wine bottle labels. Assemble a wide selection of labels and compile a catalog. In your catalog also include, starter packs, albums, framed labels, etc. Collect the labels from used wine bottles from wine bars and hotels.

700.   Start a seasonal business which sells bulbs door-to-door. This business is best operated by two people: one calls on houses and the other moves a handcart full of bulbs.

701.   Paint attractive art on rocks to make souvenir paperweights and doorstops. The art might take the form of abstract pattern, traditional pictures or tourist scenery. Call your rocks "designer rocks". Add a rubber base to paperweights and a rubber edge to doorstops.

702.   Place classified ads in newspapers which read: 'Anything bought, Cash paid' or 'Houses cleared'. Make money from reselling what you pick up.

703.   Start an enterprise which organizes trips to sports events such as boxing contests, motor racing competitions, athletics events, etc. Your service provides the tickets and the transport. You might, for example, pay a shopkeeper to open a ticket office in his or her shop on Saturdays.

704.   Start a business which produces and sells video pets. A person buys a video about a cat or a dog and this acts as a mild substitute for the real thing. The advantages include: no feeding,

no smell or hairs around the home, and no looking after or taking out for a walk.

705.   Organize holidays for people at American farms and ranches. First advertise in the States for farmers and ranch owners who want to have paying guests. Then advertise in a variety of publications in this country for clients.

706.   Sell simple exercise and keep fit devises door-to-door.

707.   Produce an audio CD course on 'Teaching Yourself Gaelic'. Sell by mail order throughout the world.

708.   Write booklets or produce audio CDs about different aspects of making a career in the music business. For example: 'How to be an independent record producer', 'How to get a recording contract', 'How to form your own group', etc. Use small ads in the music press to attract buyers.

709.   Slice timber logs and burn letters into the wood to make house name signs. Also varnish them and sell from a stall at special markets or get examples stocked at retailers who would take orders for you.

710.   Reprint old photographs of a town and mount in attractive frames. Sell through local shops. Advertise in local press for residents who have old photographs you could pay a fee to have reproduced.

711.   Deal in butterflies and sell to collectors by post. Obtain stock by advertising your interest in buying butterfly collections in collectors magazines.

712.   Begin a business which sells original paintings on hire purchase or revolving credit. Almost everyone would like to own original oil paintings but are put off because of the high initial cost.

713.   Visit offices during lunch breaks, or before work begins, to give keep-fit classes.

714.   Design and organize the production of stop smoking penalty boxes. Every time a person smokes, he or she pays a fine. Pay a plastics injecting moldings firm to manufacture the boxes. Distribute the finished plastic boxes to wholesalers and a wide range of retailers.

715.   Use leather fabrics to make pen wallets and pencil cases. Sell the wallets and cases empty or buy pens and pencils at trade prices and fill the wallets and cases to make the finished product.

716.   Produce a questionnaire which is designed to find out if one person really loves another. Place classified ads in magazines for teenagers or women which read : 'Does he really love you?'. Send respondents a questionnaire and process it for a charge. Or design a questionnaire which can be assessed by the client.

717.   Start a mail order business which sells fund-raising accessories. For example: booklets about fund-raising ideas, bingo calling machines, scratch cards and many, many others. Produce a catalog about your goods and send it to clubs, societies, associations and schools.

718.   Put together a correspondence course about how to become a stock-market chartist. Sell through ads in financial newspapers and magazines.

719.   Found and run a school of investment. Give tuition to solo students and to groups about different types of investments such as shares, gilt-edged securities, unit trusts, USM, antiques, stamps, arts, etc. For each area covered, prepare lesson plans and follow these closely.

720.   Invent and make wooden 2-D and 3-D executive puzzles. For example: 3-D puzzles which have lots of interlocking pieces. Have them stocked at gift shops and stationers.

721.   Design and make leather stamp wallets for philatelists. These would be for keeping duplicates and stamps for sale. The wallets might vary in size from the pocket to the desktop. Sell through stamp shops and adverts in stamp magazines.

722.   Begin a crafts business which incorporates a barometer, digital clock, calendar and thermometer into a single framed picture. For example, these might be a picture of an aircraft cockpit or cityscape and set among the dials or skyscraper is the barometer, clock, etc.

723.   Publish an 'ideas' newsletter for photographers. Focus the attention of the newsletter on ideas for salable photographs. Use ads in photography magazines to sell subscriptions and emphasize that the newsletter aims to help people to earn money from photography.

724.   Invent a cartoon character which captures the spirit of your town or region. Pick a name which matches the name of the town or region. E.g. Billy Brighton, Mickey Middlesex, etc. Use this character on: T-shirts, posters, postcards, stationery, etc.

725.   Start a publishing enterprise which specializes in producing quality hand printed poetry books. Get these stocked at bookshops and sell by post to poetry lovers.

726.   Provide people dressed in unusual costumes for promotions. The costume might be specially designed to suit the corporate image of the company. Let advertising agencies and public relations departments know about your service.

727.   Create a range of desktop sea-shell products. For example: 1) Place weights inside suitable sea-shells to make paperweights. 2) use odd shaped sea-shells as 'fidget shells' to occupy restless fingers 3) sell sea-shells which have the sound of the sea as 'stress relief shells'.

728.   Begin a postal service which produces personalized bookplates. These might be printed with a persons surname, coat of arms, thematic design relating to a hobby or occupation, drawing of a home, or a portrait. Sell to people with large collections of books.

729.   In a large city operate a telephone information service for amateur photographers. Photographers who subscribe to your service can telephone you to get a list of today's photo opportunities. For example: a film star arriving at an airport and a record breaking attempt.

730.   Start a business which brings out a library of children's stories on audio CDs. Have these stocked at toy shops and bookshops or start a monthly club.

731.   Put together a mail order service which sells rocks and mineral specimens to collectors. Produce a catalog which lists a

wide range of minerals and rock specimens. Also include in the catalog collectors supplies and accessories.

732.   Hire out brass-ware for decorating the reception areas of businesses such as pubs, hotels, restaurants, hair salons, offices, etc. Also, some custom might come from householders who are keen on brass-ware.

733.   Produce a library of audio CDs about the history of world war II. The advantage of these CDs is that they can feature the sounds of historic events. Have them stocked at shops which sell books or records or bring out a catalog and set up a mail order business.

734.   Sell mounted etchings by calling on private households and shopkeepers. Buy from the original artist or from a wholesaler.

735.   Package selections of empty matchboxes. Distribute these to newsagents to sell to children who collect empty matchboxes. Or get them stocked at specialists collectors outlets such as stamp and modeling shops.

736.   Earn money from selling house numbers and name signs door-to-door. Houses often have rusty, old or difficult to see numbers. This presents an excellent opportunity for a direct sales business.

737.   Begin a lesson of the month club for those who want to learn the principles of management. Each lesson takes the form of a newsletter. The lessons are strung together to make a complete management course.

738.   Design and make doll's clothes for collectors or manufacturers of dolls. Either make the clothes to order or produce a mail order catalog which gives full detail of your range.

739.   Arrange holiday exchanges between various English speaking nationalities such as English, Scottish, Americans, Australians and Canadians. You might either provide a personal service which matches people or publish a newsletter listing people seeking exchanges.

740.   Sell products related to the game of bridge by mail order. Conduct a world-wide search for products related to bridge. Produce a catalog and advertise in up-market national publications.

741.   Be a professional family affairs adviser. Just as a careers adviser gives advice on career improvement and development, your service gives advice on improving the future of an entire family. The advice might be about finance, careers, education, relationships, etc.

742.   Bring out a correspondence course which gives instruction about becoming a professional researcher. This course would appeal to those who would like a career in this field and to authors who want to do their own research. Sell from ads in literary publications.

743.   Compile and publish a directory of sales messages, phrases and selling points. The format of this directory might be copyright free art clipping books. All businesses are potential buyers. Sell by direct mail.

744.   Produce a correspondence course which teaches about how to trace your own ancestry. Call your business a 'School of Ancestral Research'. Advertise in a wide range of publications.

745.   Set up a mail order business which sells kits for making leather products. For example, kits for wallets, checkbook covers and pension book covers. Design and manufacture the kits yourself and produce a catalog.

746.   Start a mail order company which sells business equipment and accessories for left-handed people. Bring out a catalog and send it to large and medium-sized businesses.

747.   Begin a business which rents out large and expensive astronomical telescopes to householders who want to develop their interest in astronomy. Publicize your service at the local astronomy society and use local advertising to attract clients.

748.   Place racks of bead necklaces at a wide range of shops. Buy the bead necklaces from importers and mount them on the racks yourself.

749.   Set up a production line which sells besom brooms. The brush part of the broom is made from twigs. Obtain your supply of twigs from the waste material produced by tree surgeons. Get your brooms stocked at garden centers and hardware shops.

750.   Open and run a school of money-management. Give tuition to classes and solo students. Teach students about the techniques, attitudes and systems which can be used for the effective management of money. Students should find the cost of your course more than pays for itself.

751.   Commission an artist to do a contemporary map of your town or region in the style of maps from antiquity. Produce and frame prints of this map. Distribute to shops throughout the region.

752.   Set up a production line which turns out mini-gardens in bowls and pots. Sell from your own market stall or through a range of retail outlets.

753.   If you have the artistic ability to become a cartoon caricaturist, earn money from doing amusing portraits at a thoroughfare of a shopping or tourist area. Or do caricatures outside football grounds on match day, at festivals, concerts, exhibitions, etc.

754.   Design and make wooden wheels of fortune. Produce in a variety of sizes and designs. Sell or hire as fund-raising aids to clubs, associations, schools and colleges.

755.   Give tuition in your own home to those who want to improve their spoken English. There is a vast pool of clients as most people would like to become more articulate. Use local advertising to attract students.

756.   Bring out a range of T-shirts to distribute to bookshops, record-shops, computing shops, gift shops or newsagents. The design on the T-shirts might be aimed at the customers of the shops they appear in, for example, a literary theme for bookshops.

757.   Start a business which specializes in writing sales letters. Call on small businesses to sell your service and show samples of

your work. Your service should be good enough to improve the sales pull of almost any sales letter a firm already has.

758.   Design and organize the printing of 'for sale' signs for car owners who want to sell their car. These will have a brightly colored backing and are placed in the car windows by the owner. Arrange for signs to be stocked at car accessory shops.

759.   Supply life extension products by post. Model your business on similar businesses which have been successful in the USA. Obtain a catalog from one of these businesses and base your business on their system.

760.   Produce an audio CD training course about salesmanship. The object of the course might be to bring out and develop the salesperson in anyone. For this reason almost everyone is a potential buyer.

761.   Use lace to make unusual jewelery, such as lace bracelets, lace earrings, brooches and necklaces. Let your imagination run wild to create the design of each item of jewelery. For example, embed lace in clear plastic.

762.   Start a pen pal club for children and adults who have an interest in literature. Members of the club can write to each other about books they read. Advertise in literary publications.

763.   Make small and attractive mosaics for hanging on walls like paintings. For example, a mosaic might be circular and feature the face of a goddess from the ancient world.

764.   Call door-to-door and offer to take top quality passport photographs. Take the photographs in the customers house.

Someone returns at a later date to deliver the photographs and collect payment. All family members might have their photos taken for passports, ID cards, bus and train passes, etc.

765.   Use prints of lunar or Martian landscapes to make unusual framed prints or posters.

766.   Begin a mail order business which sells stencil craft. Make stencils which can be used by woodworkers, for example, to add attractive designs to their work. A stencil might depict flowers and a woodworker would use paint or ink to imprint the design onto their work.

767.   Start a second-hand art bookstall and take it to antique markets or fairs. Obtain your stock by placing ads in art or book collectors magazines. State that you wish to buy collections of second-hand art books.

768.   Organize theme parties for children and teenagers. You supply the party-goers with simple costumes, food and entertainment. Each party might be related to a popular theme such as science fiction, pirates, witches and wizards, Wild West, etc.

769.   Embroider exotic designs on disco and party clothes. Arrange for your work to be stocked at up-market boutiques.

770.   Design and produce craft kits for making ornaments or relief pictures with ball bearings. Get these stocked in shops or advertise in crafts magazines.

771.   Set up a school of motor racing. Offer potential students a weekend or week-long course about the practical and theoretical aspects of motor racing.

772.   Begin an enterprise which organizes day trips to race-courses. You might, for example, set up a service which leaves a city center at a regular time each day and travels to one of the race-courses open on that day.

773.   Take suitable sea-shells and sell them as sleep shells. Those who have difficulty in sleeping at night listen to a sleep shell. The soothing sound of the sea will aid sleep.

774.   Earn money by selling cacti door-to-door. Carry them in a cinema usherette-type tray.

775.   Use direct mail to sell model steam engines to engineers, doctors, scientists, company directors and other professional people.

776.   Market a short or toy tug-of-war rope. Package the rope and get it stocked at sports or toy shops respectively. A short rope for adults and a toy rope for children could be used to play small scale games of tug of war. Or the rope could be attached to a wall to make an exercise device.

777.   Start a school of stock market investment. With the number of shareholders growing there is a growing demand for tuition about investing in the stock market. Hold classes at home and in hired offices and halls. Also do a correspondence course or a lesson of the month newsletter.

778.   Take mechanical things like locks or gears. Cut them in half or remove the outer casing. Mount what you have left to make unusual ornaments. You might, for example, buy used and obsolete locks and gears from engineering companies.

779.   Set up a service which supplies sliced and seeded lemons to pubs, restaurants, night-clubs and hotels. In the course of an evening some bars use a large quantity of sliced lemons. These establishments could benefit from the convenience of having the lemons ready-sliced.

780.   Sell unusual musical instruments from your own catalog, by post. For example: folk music instruments from Third World countries, and early musical instruments.

781.   At a seaside resort set up a seasonal business which organizes boat trips and day-long coach excursions for holiday-makers. The boat and coaches will be hired from local operatives and you can sell tickets from camping site shops, newsagents and tourist information centers.

782.   Produce photographs about one inch square of the human eye. Frame each photograph. Sell each framed eye as a novelty for sticking on a wall or door. This novelty can be unnerving because it creates the impression that someone is watching through a hole in the wall or door.

783.   Take metal rods and tubes of different diameters and cut into slices. Arrange the slices to make pictures and patterns. Mount these pictures and sell as craft work. Or produce kits for making pictures with slices of rods and tubes. Use mail order to sell these kits to craft-workers.

784.   Design, produce and distribute tie clips which have a theme related to astrology, football, a holiday resort, etc.

785.   Organize the production of photographic business cards and sell these direct to businesspeople. You might also produce blank photographic business cards for printers. For example a card features a photograph which is representative of a trade, a printer would print personal details next to the picture.

786.   Run an international pop music pen pal club. Produce a quarterly publication which lists people looking for pen pals. Also boost your income by selling advertising space in your publication. Use small ads world-wide to recruit subscribers.

787.   Start a postal school of the cinema. Compile a variety of courses about different genres of the cinema such as westerns, science fiction and musicals. Produce a prospectus and advertise in cinema and film magazines.

788.   Organize weekend breaks where individuals can have their career assessed by professional career advisers. Advice should also be given on how to develop a career or how to make a change. Advertise in up-market or business publications.

789.   Design and make herb gardens for the house or garden. Produce the herb gardens in a range of different containers such as bottles, tubs, trays, large pots or hanging pots. Sell through suitable retailers or by mail order.

790.   Start a school of psychic phenomena and the unknown. Offer potential students easy-to-do postal courses on subjects such as UFO's, sea monsters, ghosts, etc. Advertise in a wide range of publications.

791.   Sell cheap labor saving devices door-to-door, for example: potato peelers, chip cutting machines, easy-to-use can openers, etc.

792.   Begin a mail order firm which sells personalized everyday objects such as pens, towels, handkerchiefs, notepads, combs, etc. Produce a catalog and advertise in up-market publications. Offer customers hampers of personalized products.

793.   Organize courses about how to build your own house extension or loft conversion. Hold the courses during the weekends at the construction site of an extension or conversion. Or a bed and breakfast house could be hired out of season for a week-long course.

794.   Design and produce a range of amusing self-adhesive stickers for children. The stickers might feature jokes, funny faces and streetwise statements. Distribute to wholesalers, newsagents and toy shops.

795.   Have a market stall which sells cosmetics. Cosmetics usually have good profit margins and a market stall has low overheads. These two factors combined make it an attractive business opportunity.

796.   Serve coin collectors by starting a coin or coin of the month club. Activities might include sending collectors new foreign coins as they are issued.

797.   Start a slide set of the month club for collectors of slides. Slides might be about, for example, classic photographs, art, technology, airplanes, trains and stamps. Advertise in photography magazines.

798.   Start a vegetarian food catering service. Devise a menu with imaginative meals. Advertise in political and environmental publications.

799.   Manufacture marbles draughts sets. Instead of a checkerboard there is a wooden board with 64 round holes. The holes become the squares of the draughtboard and the marbles sit in them. Each side has marbles of a different color and some extra colors to use as 'kings'.

800.   In districts with numerous offices, factories or shops, organize an after work dating service. Send leaflets about your service and membership application forms to all the work places in a district.

801.   Begin a business which invents, produces and distributes role-playing board games. This field is not as competitive as other board games and if a game can gain a reputation role-playing game enthusiasts will be willing buyers.

802.   Use wooden jigsaw pieces to make earrings and necklaces. Add a hand painted design to the side of the jigsaw piece not covered by a part of the picture. Call your goods jigsaw puzzle jewelery. Sell from a stall at fairs, car boot sales or get it stocked at trendy shops.

803.   Find a source of common or high-quality soil, package and sell through hardware shops and garden centers.

804.   With the permission of the appropriate authority, if needed, sell nuts in an open space of a city center to passers-by and tourists for feeding the pigeons. Or, at a suitable seaside

resort, sell bits of fish to holiday-makers who want to feed the seagulls.

805.   Start a mail order business which sells vitamin pills. Produce a catalog which contains a far wider range of vitamin pills than is available at shops.

806.   Start a business which rents out drum kits and electric guitars. Advertise your business both in the local press and in the windows of newsagents. Provide a delivery service.

807.   Bring out an audio CD course about how to be assertive at home and at work. Use direct mail to sell the course to businesspeople and opportunity seekers.

808.   Design and manufacture portable mini-golf courses. Each hole on the course might consist of a large, colorful wooden sheet which has pop-up features like a pop-up book. Nine sheets will fit in a van. Sell or hire for fund raising and money-making.

809.   Found your own institute of beauty. This institute would be the beauty world's equivalent to : 1) a finishing school (for women who want to become expert in doing their own make up) and 2) a secretarial school. (for women who want a career in the beauty industry.)

810.   Set yourself up in business as a music concert promoter. Approach a local pop or rock group and offer to organize a gig for them. If your first gig is successful slowly work your way up in the concert promoting business.

811.   Bring out a correspondence course about creative thinking and attract students by advertising in national newspapers and

magazines. The ads might have a headline like 'Do people say you lack imagination?', or 'The amount of money you make is limited only by your imagination'.

812.   Organize outdoor holidays in America. For example, walking or cycling holidays in the Rockies. Sell places on these holidays to people in Britain and the rest of Europe.

813.   Design and manufacture kits for making unusual furniture. For example: tables that hang from the ceiling, chairs with odd shapes, stylistic plant stands, etc. Produce a catalog about your product and start a mail order business.

814.   Produce and distribute a selection of ashtrays which feature the face of a hated person. Every time a smoker finishes a cigarette they stub it out in the face of the hated person.

815.   At a crafts fair or market, operate a jewelery lucky dip. Bring together a selection of enameled, sea-shell, bead and carved jewelery in a box. Wrap the box and place in a large tub of sawdust. Passers by are invited to pick a box for a small charge.

816.   Set up a school of variety entertainment. Teach beginners about the variety entertainment business. Also show beginners how to improve any acts of their own which they would like to perform.

817.   Produce vanity poetry audio CDs or DVDs. Pay a celebrity to read a poet's work to a video camera, or make a recording on audio tape. Your service might also include producing copies of the recording on audio or video for distribution.

818.   Start an enterprise which delivers table flowers on a regular basis to : restaurants, hair salons, dental surgeries, offices, etc. Call on these places to sell your services.

819.   Bring out a correspondence course about how to compose and write hymns. Advertise in the religious press. Also arrange for agents in foreign countries to sell the course.

820.   Manufacture Australian cork hats. These hats might be a cheap novelty version of the real thing. Sell these cork hats through shops which sell novelties, souvenirs or gifts. Or import real cork hats from Australia and use ads in magazines to sell these by mail order.

821.   Start a newsletter on how to get a better job. Provide subscribers with advice on where to look, completing application forms, interview techniques, C.V. preparation, etc. The competitive nature of the job market means that the extra advice provided by your newsletter could make all the difference to a job applicants success.

822.   Make pendants from sea-shells. Use gold paint to highlight the features of each shell. Or use ordinary paints for pictures or patterns on each shell. Sell through gift or souvenir shops or from a market stall.

823.   Collect seaweed. Use this in a seaweed weather forecasting kit of your own design. Use mail order to sell the kits. Also discover how seaweed can be developed into a health food and start a business exploiting this opportunity.

824.   Set up a mail order business which sells gold chain by the inch. Use creative advertising to put across your sales message.

825.   Start an international correspondence club for stamp collectors. The benefits of membership would include being able to swap stamps, magazines, books and information. Match stamp collectors according to their interests and produce a periodic publication for all members.

826.   Seek out the most powerful magnifying glass in the world. Buy numerous of these at trade prices and start a mail order business with your product as the 'World's Most Powerful Pocket Magnifying Glass'.

827.   Give personal tuition in your own home on how to write good English. Advertise your service by placing cards in windows of local newsagents. Point out the advantages of taking the course, such as getting a better job and helping the children with their homework.

828.   Bring out a product which consists of lots of small colored wooden cubes. These can be used over and over again to make mosaics. Have this product stocked at shops or sell by mail order.

829.   Begin a business which organizes specialist adventure holidays for women. The holidays should be designed to help women develop their skills and abilities related to: management, persuasiveness, problem solving, leadership, creative thinking, etc.

830.   Begin a lesson of the month club for those who want to start a business. Each lesson would be like a monthly newsletter and would be part of a comprehensive course. The lessons might be about starting a business either in general, or about a specific type of business such as mail order or retailing.

831.   Bring out a careers guide to self-employment. Sell this through as many bookshops as possible. Hopefully this guide will become an annual publication which will appeal to a new crop of people every year.

832.   Start a production line which turns out hand-painted wooden egg cups for selling at shops. Or at a market stall paint personalized egg cups while the buyer waits.

833.   Start a knitting patterns of the month club. Each month, members of your club automatically receive a selection of the latest knitting patterns. Members select the patterns they want and return the rest. Or compile a top 30 of patterns and send new entries to club members.

834.   Begin a mail order business which sells hydroponics growers supplies(hydroponics is a method of growing plants without soil). Produce a catalog and advertise in gardening publications.

835.   Start a mail order business which sells new and second-hand Jazz records. Many rare and classic Jazz records are released in overseas countries. Import these to sell to collectors in this country. Also locate overseas sources of second-hand records.

836.   Design and manufacture skin painting kits. In each kit have a spectrum of colors and a selection of designs which can be easily copied. Get your kits stocked at shops which sell toys, novelties or artists materials.

837.   Start a service which organizes the painting of murals in bedrooms, dining rooms, residential games rooms, etc. Advertise in up-market publications.

838.   Publish a newsletter about cocktail drinks. In each issue include: information about new and classic cocktail drinker tips, the best way to make drinks, new cocktails which you devise yourself, etc. Your market includes all businesses licensed to sell drinks.

839.   Manufacture wooden snooker score-boards for professional and amateur players. Try to bring out an inexpensive score-board which can be sold to players who have a snooker table in their own home.

840.   Design your own unique brand of cat scratch posts. For example, if you have a cat which scratches an armchair or wall, base your design on this. Make, package and distribute your scratch posts to suitable retailers or sell by post.

841.   Design and produce a series of wall charts for children. One chart might ask a child to record one good deed a day; another might ask a child to record new words learnt; a third might be for recording the weather or what happened at school.

842.   Start a mail order firm which sells live insects, insectaria and other products related to keeping and breeding insects. Advice might also be given on what insects to keep. Your service might be called 'Select an Insect'. Also publish a newsletter with a title like 'Insect Keeper'.

843.   Begin a service which organizes a telephone chess playing club. A member might have four chess boards and pieces next to the phone. When a member has worked out his move on each board, he telephones his opponent.

844.   If you're good with figures, you could begin a book keeping service. Small business owners would welcome someone else balancing the books and keeping the paperwork in order,

845.   Start a van sales and delivery business which works for importers and small manufacturers. Build up a complimentary range of products from different importers and manufacturers and call on potential customers. Examples of product ranges are health foods, hobby supplies, sportswear and electrical goods.

846.   Start a business which makes a range of quality old-fashioned long johns. Produce a catalog and start a mail order business.

847.   Make a series of cookery instruction videos. These should teach people how to make all kinds of dishes and foods. Start a postal business to rent or sell these videos.

848.   Design and make a range of fishing lures at home. Sell these by getting them stocked at fishing tackle shops, starting a monthly club which sends anglers one of the latest fishing lures and giving the lures an appealing name like 'lucky charm lures'.

849.   Put together a humorous mail order package which sells products that describe the afterlife. For example, produce a series of audio CDs which describe exactly what it's like in heaven and hell.

850.   Start a venture which designs and manufactures portable theater footlights. Potential buyers include: amateur theater and dance groups, rock groups, children's entertainers, variety entertainers, nightclubs and mobile disk jockeys.

851.   Create a mail order business which sell sensory exploration kits for young children. Make many of the kits yourself. For example, one kit might consist of a wide range of colors on different cards, another might have a wide range of rough and smooth materials.

852.   At a crafts fair or antiques market have a stall which sells products related to Shakespeare. These might include: prints, books, audio CDs, videos and posters.

853.   Write and publish a series of booklets on how to turn various hobbies into businesses, for example, 'How to start an electronics business'. Other hobbies might include: stamp or book collecting, photography, angling, and video making. Sell through ads in hobby and business opportunity magazines.

854.   Sell cheap toys door-to-door. Visit neighborhoods which have an above average population of children.

855.   Set up a bead craft-work business. Use beads to make a selection of jewelery such as necklaces, pendants, bracelets and earrings. Sell from a market stall or mount on display racks and get shops to stock them.

856.   Set up an enterprise which manufactures hutches and coops for small animals, birds and poultry. Sell in kit or finished form by mail order.

857.   Sell pillowcases printed with amusing designs and statements relating to popular themes, such as football, romance and sex. For example, one amusing design might be related to the Kama Sutra and a witty statement might be 'The center forward of Liverpool and a score every time'.

858.   Earn money from selling badges at pop concerts, festivals, tourist sites and other places where there are crowds.

859.   Produce a correspondence course about cartooning. Pay a skilled cartoonist to devise the course.

860.   Open your own school of drama. Prepare a simple prospectus which offers a comprehensive introduction to drama. Hold classes in a hired hall. Also visit businesses and clubs to give classes during lunch hours.

861.   Start a crafts business which makes unusual table lamps. Each lamp might feature a stand made of a conch shell, for example, or a Victorian bottle. If you hit upon a design which is popular, and their are no problems for obtaining raw materials, this can become a full-time business.

862.   Put together a range of spoken word audio CDs. Have them stocked in video rental shops and rented out as an alternative to a video.

863.   Begin a mail order business which sells things related to cult figures such as Nikola Tesla, L. Ron Hubbard, Leonardo Da Vinci, John Lennon, James Dean, etc. Sell things such as press cuttings, photographs, audio CDs, books, etc.

864.   Publish a newsletter for separated and divorced people. Discuss issues relevant to being separate or divorced. Also include classified listings of people who are looking for new partners.

865.   Start a universal correspondence club. This club should be able to boast that it can find someone to correspond about any

subject. Produce a leaflet about your club and list many subjects. Recruit club members by placing classified ads in a diversity of publications at home and abroad.

866.   Canvass shops for older, soiled or other unwanted stock and offer to buy it at a nominal sum. No one else is likely to buy the stock so this is probably the only opportunity the owner has to sell it. Hire a hall and sell the stock at low prices to the public. Or sell at a car boot sale or from a market stall.

867.   Begin a business which makes and distributes souvenir lucky charms. One example is a number seven made from metal and stamped with a place name.

868.   Produce an audio CD course or correspondence course about entrepreneurship. The potential market includes the hundreds of thousands of people who start their own business each year.

869.   Make leather and wooden souvenir luggage tags. These tags might feature the name of a holiday town and a popular scene. Get your tags stocked at shops visited by tourists.

870.   Organize the production of concrete or plastic garden gnomes and statues. Have them stocked at garden centers and retailers who sell garden products.

871.   Manufacture mosaic garden ornaments. These ornaments feature a mosaic picture in the design. They might include mosaic stepping stones, mosaic bird baths and mosaic sundials. A mosaic ornament adds to a garden a touch of the ancient world.

872.   Call on regular clients once every eight weeks to sell cosmetics. The cosmetics should have a special feature, for example, they do not involve cruelty to animals, or are based on herbs.

873.   Start a business which makes a range of souvenir or commemorative wall plaques. They might have a feature such as: town crests, tourist maps, commemorative statements or logos, etc. Sell your wall plaques through gift shops and hotels.

874.   Organize pop or rock music talent contests. The income from each contest would come from either, charging the performers an entrance fee or selling tickets to the public. You may even be able to find a sponsor to back the entire contest.

875.   Hand paint nostalgic scenes and old advertisements on mirrors. Sell through gift shops or from a market stall.

876.   Take up the craft of jewelery making and as soon as you acquire a basic skill, start selling what you make. Begin by sending for a catalog issued by a mail order jewelery making supplier.

877.   Rent out scaffolding for exterior home decorating and maintenance. Advertise in local newspapers and newsagents windows. Provide a free delivery service.

878.   Write and publish a manual about how to make money from buying bankrupt stock. Sell this to business opportunity seekers by direct mail or classified ads.

879.   Research, write and produce a manual or correspondence course about 'How to start your own holiday organizing

business'. This might cover everything from organizing walking holidays to conventional sightseeing holidays. Sell to opportunity seekers.

880.   Sell parcels of unsorted books by post to book collectors. Or offer second-hand books for sale by the foot. Obtain your stock by buying books which cannot be sold from second-hand book dealers and publishers.

881.   Begin a direct mail or mail order business which sells crafts books to craft workers. Buy books from publishers, buy manuscripts from authors and publish these yourself, or write a craft book which has universal appeal and sell this.

882.   Start a children's record or audio CD of the month club. The records and CDs sold by the club might be educational, stories or music.

883.   Operate a children's lucky dip at markets and crafts fairs. This would consist of a box of wood shavings mixed with small toys in wrapping paper. A child or their parent pays a standard charge, for example, one pound and the child takes out a wrapped toy.

884.   Begin a party plan business which sells self-instruction and 'how to' books, CDs and courses. Add a competitive edge to the business by producing many of the products yourself.

885.   Devise quizzes which test a persons vocabulary. Sell these to a magazine or newspaper on a regular basis. Alternatively you might do quizzes which test a persons knowledge of a regional dialect. Sell these to regional papers or magazines.

886.   Set up a business which invents toys for pets. Most cat owners love to use cotton, wool, string or paper to play games with their pets. This shows a gap in the market exists. A toy which proves popular with cats has huge sales potential. Also, there is always room for a good new toy for dogs.

887.   Begin a crafts enterprise which turns out wire craft ornaments. These ornaments are free-standing, 3-D objects which consist entirely of wire: the wire makes the outlines. The ornaments might be in the shape of: airplanes, helicopters, people, animals, boats or bicycles.

888.   Place small ads in various overseas business and trade magazines which read 'I want to buy adult X-rated products suitable for selling by mail order'.

889.   Start a business which designs and manufactures DIY kits for building small garden swimming pools. Offer buyers a selection of sizes and sell through ads in DIY magazines.

890.   Take an ordinary magnifying glass, package it and call it 'The Gardener's Magnifying Glass'. Distribute to hardware shops or sell by mail from ads in gardening magazines.

891.   Make a toffee of your own design and add a stick to make a toffee lollipop. Get them stocked at newsagents and confectioners or sell from a stall at markets, fairs and exhibitions.

892.   Set up a postal business which hires out replicas of rifles and pistols. Your main custom would come from gun collectors and amateur theatrical producers.

893.   Bring out a selection of pretty, non-picture postcards which are specially designed for friends to send brief notes to each other. Have them stocked at stationers, newsagents and shops which sell greeting cards.

894.   Design and make kits for making soft toy dolls. Place ads in craft magazines and sell by mail order.

895.   If you have the skill, work as a charcoal artist in a thoroughfare of a shopping or tourist area.

896.   Start an enterprise which reproduces classic poems on postcards and posters. Also do framed prints of classic poems. Sell these from a stall in an antiques or crafts market or get them stocked at souvenir or gift shops.

897.   Start a semi-professional theater group which earns money from performing at private parties, business promotions, tourist sites and public events.

898.   Bring out an audio CD library of limericks. This might be produced for children or young adults. Have the CDs stocked at bookshops, toy shops and newsagents.

899.   Set up a company which produces a compendium of strip games, for example: Strip poker, strip snakes and ladders, strip lotto, strip snap, and strip ludo. Sell by mail order from adverts in X-rated magazines.

900.   Become a professional organizer of private and business parties. You provide clients with a comprehensive service which does everything from supplying caterers to organizing a coat

checking service. Advertise your service in a wide variety of publications.

901.   Design and produce a selection of astrological badges for each star sign. Place these badges on cards or boards and distribute them to suitable retailers.

902.   Become a street or market craft-worker. Sit at a stall making, for example, ornaments from wire or shells. Display the goods you make on your stall. The act of making the ornaments attracts the curiosity of passers-by. This should result in a respectable level of sales.

903.   Package low value foreign coins in cellophane envelopes. Distribute these coins to newsagents for selling to children in the way small packets of stamps are sold.

904.   Bring out a correspondence course about how to write screenplays for feature films. There is obviously a lot of skill involved in writing a screenplay and there are numerous people who would be willing to pay to learn.

905.   Produce a series of low cost audio CDs which help school pupils revise for public examinations. You might give these CDs a brand name like 'Personal School Revision CDs". Get them stocked at newsagents and bookshops.

906.   Set up a business which produces X-rated jigsaw puzzles. These might be sold either by mail order or, to wholesalers of X-rated products.

907.   Use classified ads to sell a selection of English language newspapers from around the world. Buyers will include those

who are curious about what overseas English language newspapers are like.

908.   Begin an enterprise which sells garden gates door-to-door. On your sales trip take with you a smart folder which has a large photograph of each gate you are selling. Provide potential customers with a price which includes installation.

909.   Produce writing paper which has borders printed with pretty rural scenery or flowers. Get this stocked at stationers and tourist shops.

910.   Put together a correspondence course about how to become an amateur magician. The aim would be teach people who to do numerous basic tricks. It would be a foundation course for amateur magicians. Also sell the products that magicians tricks require.

911.   Research, write and publish a series of booklets about how to start and run specific home businesses. Examples of titles might include: 'Money from Typing at Home', 'Your Own Telephone Sales Business', 'Your Own Knitting Business', etc. Sell by mail order.

912.   Have T-shirts printed with sci-fi messages on the front such as 'Alpha Centauri University', Visit Ancient Egypt with TWA's Time Travel Tours', 'Test fly a Centauri flying saucer, visit your local dealer', etc. Sell at sci-fi conventions and through sci-fi shops.

913.   Start a service which cleans wire baskets and supermarket trolleys. Baskets and trolleys often spend most of the day on a dusty floor or outside, open to the elements.

914.   Arrange for greeting messages to be carved into stone. Sell at shops as an everlasting version of greeting cards. Or start a postal service which turns out personalized greetings in stone.

915.   Write and publish a newsletter about how to start a newsletter publishing business. Each issue of the newsletter might be a lesson about one of the various topics involved in beginning and running a successful newsletter.

916.   During the Christmas period, sell holly and mistletoe door-to-door.

917.   Produce a selection of key-rings which have unusual fobs. For example the fobs might be made from: large flat sea-shells, large foreign coins, circles cut from old LPs, fossils, slate, etc. Sell from a stall at crafts fairs and flea markets.

918.   Learn how to make china dolls and once your work reaches a high standard make an income from teaching others. Hold classes in your own area or devise a postal course.

919.   Devise a programme which is designed to make a person more dynamic. A more dynamic, confident person has a greater chance of achieving success in life. Publish your programme and sell it by direct mail to business opportunity seekers.

920.   Set yourself up as a freelance photographer by finding an unusual way into the business. One idea is to go to one of the many gold rushes around the world and do photo studies. Another idea is to visit a war in a third-world country. One good photo will sell to publications world-wide.

921.   Stain sawdust with different colors of ink. Fill clear bottles and jars with the colored sawdust so that attractive patterns are made. Also pictures can be built up on the sides of bottles if different colors are carefully arranged. Sell as souvenirs or ornaments.

922.   Make a selection of leather wallets for playing cards. For example, a pocket wallet or a wallet for attaching to a belt. Include a pack of playing cards in each wallet. Have them stocked at a wide range of shops.

923.   Begin a business which deals in old and new American and British comics. This business might: 1) Sell comics by post from a catalog. 2) Operate a comics of the month club for specialized collectors and 3) Run a comics stall at fairs and markets.

924.   Write and produce a series of audio CDs about the many aspects of sex education. Have a catalog printed and start a mail order business.

925.   Use wood to make desktop stands for holding reference books such as dictionaries, trade directories, map books and telephone directories. Have these stocked at bookshops and stationers or sell by mail order.

926.   In a tourist area open a market stall where you can print personalized T-shirts on the spot. Or start a mail order service which prints personalized T-shirts. If screen printing is used all the equipment can be made at home. Obtain and read books about screen printing to get the know-how.

927.   Put together a home study course about the technical aspects of film making. This course might be the cornerstone of your own postal film school. Sell from ads in film magazines.

928.   Start a flowers of the week, month or quarter club. Clients can place a standing order with you for the delivery of flowers at regular intervals.

929.   Take everyday objects such as clocks, water taps and calculators. Remove the outer casing and mount them to make educational aids or ornaments. Also you might label the most important parts of each object.

930.   Make concrete mini-models of cows. Each model is painted to look like a real cow. These cows are for gardeners to put on lawns to evoke the atmosphere of the countryside. Get them stocked at as many garden centers as possible.

931.   Design and produce a selection of amusing 'Keep Your Distance' car bumper stickers. For example: 'Keep your distance, or we might meet by accident', or 'Keep car mechanics poor, keep your distance'. Have them stocked at car accessory shops and service stations.

932.   Organize courses about how to increase the profitability of a bed and breakfast business. Hold these courses at holiday resorts where there are large numbers of bed and breakfast houses.

933.   Be a roadside fortune-teller.

934.   Obtain quantities of sand from the beaches of the D-day invasion. Place the sand in tiny bottles and sell world-wide as

souvenir sand from the beaches of the 1944 D-day invasion. Add a name label to each bottle to show which beach the sand came from.

935.   Have your own fabrics market stall and sell ordinary fabrics, rolls of discontinued lines and remnants.

936.   Start a newspaper and magazine roadside stand. Ask established newspaper vendors how they got started.

937.   Select one sea-shell which would be suitable for an ashtray, another for a pip tray and another for a paper clip tray. Put these shells into a single packet and sell as a set of useful sea-shell-trays. Sell from souvenir and novelty gift shops.

938.   Bring out a card index box which has reprinted cards for holding different kinds of information. This is a card index version of personal organizers, instead of carrying around a pocket folder of information, everything is held on pre-printed cards in a desktop card index box.

939.   Use soft toy materials to make a puppet-like toy which gives children their medicine. A small soft toy has a clip attached to one hand. A parent puts the spoonful of medicine into the clip and controls the hand so that it appears that the puppet is giving the medicine. Sell by mail order through ads in women's magazines.

940.   Take an attractive photograph of a large office block. Frame enlarged copies and sell these to people who work there. This would make a good sideline business if you work in an office block and you meet many other office workers in the course of the day.

941.   Devise 'crack the code' quizzes and sell to newspapers and magazines. One example of this type of quiz is a statement where the letters of each word are replaced by different letters of the alphabet.

942.   Use a computer or word processor to provide a letter and manuscript typing service. Customers would be students, academics, small business people and tradesmen.

943.   Become a calligrapher of poems. Earn money from calligraphing poems to commission for poets and sweethearts. a) Classic poems like 'Desiderata', 'Charge of the Light Brigade', etc, and selling them as gift products. b) Poems of local origin and selling them as souvenirs.

944.   Bring out a range of cake decorations which have a football theme. Use these as the basis of a mail order business, or get them stocked by wholesalers of cake decorations.

945.   Reprint old geographical maps. Use the reprints to decorate unfinished stock bought from manufacturers. For example: desk sets, book ends, memo pads, letter racks, lamp holders, book ends, coasters, dinner mats, etc. Alternatively frame the maps in a stylish frame and sell as wall decorations.

946.   Set up a promotional sheet music publishing business. People who write music and lyrics would find it easier to sell their compositions if they were published. Published compositions could then be circulated to people in the music business.

947.   At a suitable market open a stall which is devoted to selling products devoted to a particular popular cartoon character.

948.   Locate a source of fresh, pure mud and package it in specially sealed containers. Sell this by post for beauty treatment.

949.   Become a make-up consultant. Advise women on what make-up suits their individual mix of: skin shade, hair and eye colors, nose and facial shape, etc. Once you have established your consultancy, make more money by teaching others to be make up consultants.

950.   Paint, or organize the painting of, designs on T-shirts. Sell the finished T-shirts through up-market shops where the price charged will provide a reasonable income.

951.   Compile a postal course which teaches people how to cut silhouettes. The course might include instruction on how to cut all kinds of silhouettes such as landscapes, animals and people. These silhouettes can be framed or mounted to make attractive wall-hangings.

952.   Design and make, or import, kimonos. Sell by post or get them stocked at suitable retailers.

953.   Bring out a confidential newsletter which has a title like 'How to Overcome the Dissatisfactions You have with Your Life'. Provide subscribers with ideas and inspiration. Write about case studies and answer readers' questions.

954.   Buy and sell second-hand compact disks. Buy collections of disks by post and use local ads to find sellers in your area. The

disks you acquire can be sold: by post, from a market stall, or get them stocked at local shops.

955.   Sell by direct mail to business executives a kit for practicing golf putting at the office. One idea for a selling point is that ordinary workers have a dartboard or snooker table for use during breaks, the executive needs a golf putting kit to mirror his style.

956.   Earn from doing artistic hedge cutting. Advertise in the local press and in newsagents windows. Build up a list of regular customers who need their artistic hedges maintained.

957.   Set up a mail order business which sells plans, equipment and supplies for making mosaics. Produce a catalog and advertise in crafts magazines.

958.   Design a range of first name self-adhesive stickers for children to put on their books or toys. Sell through toy shops and newsagents.

959.   Start a mail order business which sells comedy audio CDs. Obtain your stock from comedy audio CD publishers in this country and from English speaking countries overseas.

960.   Seek out English overseas language publications for teachers and educationalists. Place adverts in these publications which read: 'Educational products wanted for distribution in the UK. Write to...'.

961.   Design a standard notepad for ordering extra goods from the milkman. The notepad should have spaces for house number, date and the customers name. The rest of the notepad might

consist of a list of goods which can be ticked. Get your notepads stocked at stationers or sell them to dairies who may be willing to give them free to their customers.

962.   Prepare astrological readings and charts about family ancestors. Use astrology readings and charts to shed light on personal characteristics of ancestors. Advertise in genealogy publications.

963.   Make simple footstools - up to twelve inches in height, for standing on to reach things from shelves. Sell through local shops.

964.   Begin a postal service which hires out or sells Welsh or Gaelic spoken word audio CDs and videos. If you have a knowledge of either language, produce many of the CDs yourself.

965.   Produce a series of booklets or audio CDs about ideas for saving a variety of things. For example: 'Ideas for Saving Money', 'Ideas for Saving Time', 'Ideas for Saving You the Trouble of Dieting', etc. Sell by mail order as a complete set.

966.   Produce and sell from national publications a home study course about how to play the piano. Pay an expert pianist to devise and write the course.

967.   Establish a directory of products no longer made. This directory might include sections on toys, novelties and household goods. Design the directory for business people and inventors who want to know both what has been made before and what ideas might be revived and/or modified.

968.   Use fabrics to make soft cases for pencils, spectacles, scissors, bibles, money and other small items which are either

potentially dangerous or need protection. At first, make a diversity of products until you discover which are the most popular and profitable, then specialize.

969.   Set up a business which organizes weddings. Compile a list of tasks which need to be done to make a wedding successful. Put together a selection of packages at different prices and sell these to potential clients.

970.   If you have a porch, hold a porch sale. Raise extra cash by displaying your unwanted items at your sale.

971.   Provide yourself with a regular income by selling odd and unusual facts to all kinds of publications. For example, sell financial facts to financial magazines, football facts to football programme publishers, photography facts to photography magazines, etc.

972.   Make loveable pocket-sized soft toys and hang on a rack for display in shops. Give the toys a catchy name like 'Pocket Pets'.

973.   Use leather to make your own brand of top quality dog collars and leads.

974.   Write and publish a book about betting on horses. In this book, include details of betting systems and suggestions about how to assess the likely performance of horses. Sell copies of your book to horse racing punters from newspaper ads or by direct mail.

975.   Produce a selection of audio CDs which feature X-rated poems. Write them yourself or pay poets to write them for you. Produce a catalog and start a mail order business.

976.   Sell garden fountains to up-market householders. Produce quality sales literature and advertise in select magazines. Pay professional builders to do the building and installation work.

977.   Produce souvenir pillowcases. Each pillowcase might be printed with pictures of tourist scenery. Souvenir pillowcases have the novel feature that they help a person to relax and sleep because the pictures prompt a person to think of pleasant holiday locations.

978.   Earn money by selling gold chain by the inch at public events such as fairs, markets and exhibitions.

979.   Bring out leather and plastic belts and holsters for holding personal stereos. Arrange for these belts and holsters to be stocked at shops which sell records and audio equipment.

980.   Begin a business which organizes wildlife observation holidays. These might be based in a forest, for example, unspoiled coastal area or mountainous region. Produce a brochure and advertise in wildlife magazines.

981.   Produce and distribute souvenir boxes of matches. Each matchbox is painted with a picture postcard scene of a tourist area. Also produce a souvenir pack which contains a selection of different boxes. This pack can be bought by people as a gift or taken home for personal use.

982.   Set up a mail order business which serves the gay community. In your catalog include suitable: Books, audio CDs, videos, novelty products, posters, contact adverts section, etc.

983.   Turn large sea-shells into money boxes. Cut a slot in the shells for inserting coins and add an opening for extracting the money and block it with removable cork. These are sold as ornaments and as money boxes.

984.   Design and produce a selection of satirical, political postcards. Sell sets to collectors, retailers and political activists from ads in political publications.

985.   Begin an enterprise which makes model paper products for dolls and dolls' houses. These might include: Newspapers, money, stationery, napkins, paper hats, Christmas cards, etc. Sell these products by mail order to doll makers and collectors.

986.   Produce kits for schoolgirls to make bead necklaces. Package each kit in a small polythene bag and staple on a printed card. Mount these kits on a rack and get them displayed at newsagents.

987.   Start a spring-water bottling and distribution business. Advertise for someone who owns a property which has a natural spring water supply. Negotiate a contract with the owner which allows you to bottle and sell the spring water.

988.   Design and publish diaries for each star sign. The special feature of these diaries is that a star reading is given for each day of the coming year. Have these diaries mounted in a special display rack. Get a wide range of shops to accept your racks.

989.   Locate a source of firewood for stoves and open fires. Start a business which either packages the wood for distribution to retailers or deliver the wood direct to customers.

990.   Make peg abacuses. Each abacus is a wooden block which has rows of dots instead of beads. A row has one peg to indicate the value of that row. Package these and sell as either a children's educational aid or a novelty for adults.

991.   Produce a series of famous biographical audio CDs about famous artists, writers, politicians, inventors, film stars, etc. Sell these through bookshops or start a monthly club.

992.   Rent out large snooker tables and cues in a similar fashion to the way television sets are rented out. Rent them to householders, clubs, businesses, colleges, unions, etc.

993.   Start a music tuition agency. Offer to tutor potential students in popular musical instruments. Call your agency a school of music. Start by using advertising to recruit both part-time tutors and pupils.

994.   Bring out an information package about 'How to Start Your Own Carded Products Business' (ordinary products are mounted on card for displaying on racks or walls in shops). An information package might consist of CDs on sales dialogue, booklets and diagrams about ideas and methods.

995.   Arrange for business and personal cards to be printed which show that the holder is a dedicated supporter of a particular football team. Sell to football fans outside matches or get them stocked at suitable shops.

996.   Publish a newsletter for people who want to become children's authors. In each issue include advice and information which will help children's authors to get work accepted for publication.

997.   Use pastels or charcoals to do original pictures of tourist sites. Sell, framed or unframed, as quality souvenirs.

998.   Start an international advertising publication for philatelists. Provide dealers and collectors with an international dimension to their sales efforts and search for stamps.

999.   Produce wall-charts which helps individuals and couples manage their financial affairs. A thorough record of expenditure is made on the wall-chart. The wall-chart helps to make it easy to control finances because it is so visible to all in the household.

1000.   Start a postal service which hires out children's educational videos. A selection of videos should be offered for each age group. Produce a catalog about your videos and advertise your rental service in a wide range of publications.

Further Reading

BARRINGER, B. R., & IRELAND, R. D. (2008). *What's stopping you?: shatter the 9 most common myths keeping you from starting your own business*. Upper Saddle River, N.J., FT Press.

BEAM, L. S. (2008). *The creative entrepreneur: a DIY visual guidebook for making business ideas real*. Beverly, Mass, Quarry Books.

BEAM, L. S. (2009). *The creative entrepreneur: a DIY visual guidebook for making business ideas real*. Gloucester, Mass, Quarry.

BRABEC, B. (2002). *Handmade for profit!* New York, M. Evans and Co.

COLLINS, M. (2008). *The million-dollar idea in everyone: easy new ways to make money from your interests, insights, and inventions*. Hoboken, N.J., John Wiley & Sons.

DILLEHAY, J. (2009). *Sell your crafts online: more than 500 free and low-cost ideas for craft artists to get more links, traffic, and sales*. Torreon, NM, Warm Snow Publishers.

FOSTER, J. (2006). *How to get ideas*. San Francisco, Berrett-Koehler Publishers.

HEATH, C., & HEATH, D. (2008). *Made to stick: why some ideas survive and others die*. New York, Random House.

IZARD, M. B. (2008). *Opportunity Analysis, Business Ideas: identification and evaluation.* Lenexa, Kan, Acheve Consulting, Inc.

KADUBEC, P. (2007). *Crafts and craft shows: how to make money.* New York, Allworth Press.

KOURDI, J. (2009). *100 great business ideas: from leading companies around the world.* London, Marshall Cavendish.

LEBOEUF, M. (1997). *The perfect business: how to make a million from home with no payroll, no employee headaches, no debts, and no sleepless nights!* New York, Fireside.

STIM, R., GUERIN, L., & STIM, R. (2008). *Wow! I'm in business a crash course in business basics.* Berkeley, CA, Nolo.

www.ingramcontent.com/pod-product-compliance
Lightning Source LLC
Chambersburg PA
CBHW051526170526
45165CB00002B/618